WAR VETERANS OF UPSHUR COUNTY

By
Nathaniel Jack

McClain Printing Company
Parsons, West Virginia

1988

International Standard Book Number 0-9621648-0-1
Library of Congress Catalog Card Number 88-91439
Printed in the United States of America

To

The Veterans of Upshur County

Contents

Preface

While browsing through some old newspapers, I found some *Buckhannon Records* from the war years 1942-45. I thought it would be a good idea to take these papers to a Veterans of Foreign Wars meeting and display them.

The members were very interested in finding their own pictures and it became quite disruptive to the meeting. This proved to me that most veterans would be interested in seeing these pictures and write-ups of forty years ago during the war years.

I suggested to the membership that it would be very interesting to publish a book of veterans from Upshur County. I was made chairman of this committee, and with the cooperation of WBUC radio station and many members of VFW Post 3663, we advertised for veterans from Upshur County to help make this book a reality by bringing in their pictures and information.

I made many personal contacts and enjoyed visiting and talking to old friends and relatives of veterans. Through these contacts, I found relatives and friends of veterans from not only World War II, but from the Civil War, World War I, Korea and Vietnam. I also received much help from communities in Upshur County who sent me listings of veterans from cemeteries.

I thank the many people who supplied information to make this book possible and regret that there are some who did not supply information to be included.

Also, I thank the Veterans of Foreign Wars Post No. 3663.

Veterans of Upshur County, West Virginia

COLONEL CORNELIUS C. ("NEIL") ALBAUGH: U.S. Army—Retired. Enlisted in the 201st Infantry West Virginia National Guard in 1930 and through that service was commissioned a second lieutenant (infantry) USAR in 1936. Junior officer, camp commander and district staff officer of the Civilian Conservation Corps (CCC) 1936-1940. In December 1940 he was called to active duty, having transferred his commission to QMC in 1938. His first duty assignment was with the Ninth Quartermaster Training Regiment at Camp Lee, Virginia. In February 1942 he was transferred to the San Francisco Port of Embarkation where he served as Plans and Training officer. Feeling that he could be of more service at the newly established and expanding port of Charleston, South Carolina, he requested transfer to that port and was so assigned in September 1942, serving as assistant G-4, acting chief of staff and executive for operations. He received rapid promotions in the AUS and by November 1945, when he was assigned to the Pacific Theater of Operations (Manila), was serving in the grade of lieutenant colonel. Upon his return to the States, he served as director, Supply Division and S-4 at Fort Eustis, Virginia, for one year when he was returned to the

Col. C. C. Albaugh

Far East for duty in the Training Division and the Plans and Intelligence Division of the Transportation Section, GHQ. Integrated into the regular army in 1947, and transferred from the Quartermaster Corps to the Transportation Corps in 1950. In February 1950 he was assigned to the office, Chief of Transportation, Washington, D.C., as chief of the Continental Plans Branch, Military Plans and Intelligence. Eighteen months later he was transferred to the office, Joint Chiefs of Staff in Washington, D.C., where he served until August 1953 when he was assigned as a student at the Naval War College, Newport, Rhode Island. Upon completion of this course of instruction, he was assigned to Europe where he served as Chief, Plans and Intelligence, and executive officer of the Thirty-seventh Transportation Highway Transport Division, USAREUR, and later as transportation officer of the V Corps. While in Europe (1956), he was promoted to the grade of colonel (AUS). In April 1957 he returned to the U.S. and was assigned as transportation supply officer at the New Cumberland General Depot, Pennsylvania. November 1959 he was on his way back to the Far East. This time to the position of senior transportation advocate to the first ROK Army in Korea. Immediately following his return to the U.S. from Korea, he attended the Army Supply Management Course at the Army Logistics Management Center, Fort Lee, Virginia. Completing this course, he was assigned as deputy commander, U.S. Army Transportation Aeronautical Depot Maintenance Center (ARADMAC), NAS, Corpus Christi, Texas. On December 14, 1961, he became commanding officer of ARADMAC, the army's multimillion dollar aircraft overhaul plant. Retired from the regular army as colonel, Transportation Corps, in December 1962 after thirty years service and returning to Upshur County, where he has lived for many years. Colonel Albaugh has the following medals, badges, etc.: American Defense Service Medal, American Campaign Medal, European-African-Middle East Campaign Medal with Overseas Bar, Asiatic-Pacific Campaign Medal, Army Occupation Medal, Japan, Army Occupation Medal, Germany, World War II Victory Medal, National Defense Service Medal, Department of Defense Badge (service on JCS staff), Army

Commendation Medal with two Oak-Leaf clusters, Legion of Merit Medal.

WOODROW W. ALDERMAN: Private, Seventh Infantry, was honorably discharged from the Army of the United States on January 23, 1945, from the Army Medical Center, Washington, D.C. He was born in Alexander. He was inducted on May 10, 1943, at Clarksburg. He was a carbine expert, July 10, 1943; second class gunner, July 29, 1943 and ammunition handler, September 28, 1943. He participated in the Naples-Foggia and Rome-Arno campaigns. He was wounded in action on January 31, 1944, at Nettuno, Italy. He was awarded the Purple Heart on February 15, 1944, Expert Infantryman Badge on January 20, 1944, European-African-Middle Eastern Theater Medal with two Campaign Stars, and Good Conduct Medal on January 31, 1944. He arrived European-African-Middle Eastern Theater on November 24, 1943, and left same on April 29, 1944. He arrived in the United States on May 14, 1944.

ROBERT J. ANDEREGG: Route 4, Box 19, Buckhannon. He enlisted on October 8, 1941, and was discharged on September 19, 1945. Rating 5, he held A.S. S2C, S/C Cox BM2C. He was a local jeweler for thirty-four years.

HAROLD D. ALMOND: Captain, Forty-ninth Medical Group. He served from September 27, 1947, to August 23, 1949. He was discharged on August 23, 1949. He has been a local medical doctor for many years.

HUNTER ROOSEVELT ANDERSON: Corporal (T) on August 16, 1954. He was born November 12, 1932, in Diana. He was inducted on November 12, 1952, and was discharged on October 16, 1954. He was with Company D, Seventh Infantry Regiment. He was awarded the Korean Service Medal with one Bronze Star, United Service Medal, National Defense Service Medal, China-India-Burma Medal, and Good Conduct Medal.

P. W. Anderson

PERCY W. ANDERSON: 39 Reger Avenue, Buckhannon. He was born July 31, 1921. He enlisted in November 1940 and was discharged in November 1946 from the U.S. Navy. World War II spent in the South Pacific. Campaign Ribbons: Asiatic-Pacific-American Defense.

FERRY S. ANDERSON: First class machinist mate, U.S. Navy. He was born in Rock Cave. He was employed by the Baltimore Ship Yard. He entered the military service in February 1942. He was stationed in London, England, during World War II. He participated in the landing of the Normandy Invasion in June 1944

Ferry S. Anderson

LONNIE O'NEIL ANDREWS: Sp. 5, U.S. Army. He enlisted on July 26, 1968, and was discharged on June 26, 1974. He was awarded the National Defense Service Medal, Vietnam Service Medal, Vietnam Campaign Medal, and Army Commendation Medal. He was born on May 21, 1950, in Buckhannon.

Lonnie O'Neil Andrews

Joseph R. Andrick

JOSEPH RUSSELL ANDRICK: Airman first class, was inducted on May 10, 1958, and was discharged on August 10, 1962. He was born on October 31, 1936, in Upshur County. While in the service he was a ground radio operator and crypto operator.

BASEL TRUMAN ARBOGAST: Corporal, U.S. Army. He was inducted on January 15, 1952, and discharged on January 14, 1960. He was born on October 19, 1929, in Canaan.

Junior L. Arnold

JUNIOR L. ("BUD") ARNOLD: Joined the service in 1942 and was discharged in March 1953. He saw action in Europe and Korea. He was awarded the Good Conduct Medal, Rifleman Medal, ETO Medal, Korean Service Medal, and Distinguished Unit Citation.

ARTHUR EARNEST AUSKINGS: Sp. 4 on September 3, 1963. He was born on October 12, 1937, in Buckhannon. He was inducted on September 29, 1961. He was marksman with .45 pistol and an expert with M-1 rifle.

Left to right: Wayne, Arthur and Lawrence Auskings.

EUGENE WAYNE AUSKINGS: Sp. 5 on December 23, 1963. He was born on March 19, 1943, in Clarksburg. He joined the army on March 30, 1962. He was marksman with .45 pistol and sharpshooter with M-14 rifle.

LAWRENCE HAROLD AUSKINGS: Sergeant E-5 on June 10, 1964. He was born on November 27, 1940, in Buckhannon. He joined the army on November 22, 1961.

CARLTON R. BAILY: Entered the service on February 11, 1943, and was discharged on December 10, 1945. He lives at 187 South Kanawha Street in Buckhannon. He was an AA Air crew member. He was awarded the following badges, etc.: Carbine Sharpshooter, Ardennes-Rhyland, Central Europe, European-African-Middle Eastern Theater Ribbon with three Bronze Stars, Good Conduct Medal, Air Medal with 40LC 60374 Headquarter 3 AD 45, and Purple Heart.

FRANK BAILEY: He was born on November 24, 1908, at Hemlock. He joined the Marine Corps on September 28, 1928, and was discharged on September 17, 1932. He was awarded the Good Conduct Medal.

HAROLD T. BAILEY: Entered the service on July 24, 1918, and was discharged on March 16, 1919. He served in Bordeaux, France.

Harold Bailey

MAYFORD LYNN BAILEY: Sp.-4, U.S. Army. He was born November 1, 1945, in Buckhannon, West Virginia. He was with the Seventy-Seventh Engineering Company (PC), First U.S. Army. He was inducted on December 8, 1965, and was discharged on December 7, 1971. He received the following medals, etc.: Driver Badge, Vietnam Service Medal, Republic of Vietnam Campaign Medal with one Overseas Bar, Good Conduct Medal, National Defense Service Medal, and Marksman (rifle).

Mayford L. Bailey

Paul C. Bailey

PAUL C. BAILEY: EMC, U.S. Navy. He served his country for twenty-three years. He was honorably discharged. While serving he received the following: World War II Victory Medal, American Defense Medal, China Service Medal, Asiatic-Pacific Ribbon, Good Conduct Medal, Korean Service Medal, and United Nations Medal. Life member of VFW Post 3663.

PAUL H. BAILEY: Captain, U.S. Army (retired). Participated in campaigns in Europe. He was wounded and taken Prisoner of War at the Battle of the Bulge, Belgium. He was released from German POW Camp (X11A), Limburg, Germany, in April 1945. He retired from active duty in November 1947. He served with the Eightieth Infantry Division, Eighty-fourth Infantry Division, 542nd Parachute Battalion, Parachute School Staff, Seventeenth Airborne Division and TDY 101st Airborne Division. He received the Purple Heart, Combat Infantry Badge, Master Parachutist Badge, European Theater Ribbons with two Stars and Commendations.

Paul H. Bailey

Ronald M. Ball

RONALD M. BALL: Corporal, 122nd Chemical Processing Company. He was awarded the Good Conduct Medal, European-African-Middle Eastern Theater Ribbon with one Bronze Service Star. He joined the service on July 29, 1942, and was discharged on October 18, 1945.

Victor R. Baptista

VICTOR R. BAPTISTA: Joined the service on March 5, 1942. He served most of his military time overseas. He resides at 102 Clarksburg Road, Buckhannon, West Virginia.

JAMES M. BEER: Staff Sergeant of the Air Force, lives at 8 Marion Street, Buckhannon. He was inducted on May 13, 1942, and was discharged on October 12, 1945. He was born in Ivanhoe. Citations include: European-African-Middle Eastern Service Ribbon, Good Conduct Medal, and Distinguished Unit Badge.

James M. Beer

Maxell Lee Beer

MAXELL LEE BEER: Seaman First Class, SV6 USNR, was born on September 6, 1921, at Ivanhoe. He was inducted on August 18, 1943, and discharged on December 22, 1945.

CARL R. BENNETT: Tech. 5, U.S. Army. He enlisted on September 1, 1942. He was a marksman while serving. He was honorably discharged on October 6, 1943.

Carl R. Bennett

Emory D. Bennett

EMORY DOW BENNETT: Was in the Air Force. He was born in Upshur County. Awards included: Master Missileman Badge and Master Explosive Ordnance Disposal Badge.

SAMIE J. BROHARD: Private First Class, U.S. Army. He was born in Braxton County, West Virginia. He served with AEF in France. Sailed for AEF on May 19, 1918, and returned on July 9, 1919. The United States of America honors the memory of Samie J. Brohard. "This certificate is awarded by a grateful nation in recognition

Samie J. Brohard

of devoted and selfless consecration to the service of our country in the Armed Forces of the United States. Signed by the President of the United States—Lyndon B. Johnson."

William G. Brohard

WILLIAM G. ("BUB") BROHARD: Private First Class, 296th Signal Institute Company, U.S. Army. He was born September 18, 1923, in Brohard, West Virginia. He enlisted July 8, 1942, and was honorably discharged November 30, 1945. While serving he received the following: Good Conduct Medal, European-African-Middle Eastern Service Ribbon, American Theater Service Ribbon, and World War II Victory Ribbon.

JAMES HENRY CAMPBELL: Spec. 3 (T) in the army. He was born January 16, 1932, in Buckhannon. He joined the service on February 7, 1952, and was honorably discharged on December 26, 1954, and reenlisted on December 27, 1954, for three more years.

James H. Campbell

LEROY CANFIELD: Staff Sergeant, 3704th Army Air Force Base Unit, was discharged on October 21, 1945, from Maxwell Field, Alabama. He was born February 25, 1920, at Frenchton. He was inducted on May 13, 1942. He served in Bismarck Archipelago and New Guinea. He received the Asiatic-Pacific Ribbon with two Stars (Bronze), Good Conduct Medal, other awards.

BILLY RAY CARPENTER: Sergeant E-4, U.S. Air Force. He was born on June 25, 1948, in Buckhannon. He entered the service on December 21, 1969, and was discharged on June 6, 1972. While serving he was awarded the National Defense Service Medal, Vietnam Service Medal with one Brass Service Star, Republic of Vietnam Commendation Medal, and the Air Force Good Conduct Medal.

Billy R. Carpenter

Hubert D. Carpenter

HUBERT DENVER CARPENTER: Sergeant E5, U.S. Army. He was born on May 1, 1946, in Buckhannon. He was inducted on August 14, 1968, and was discharged on August 13, 1974. While serving he was awarded the Good Conduct Medal, National Defense Service Medal, and MKM M-14.

Hugh D. Carpenter

HUGH D. CARPENTER: Sergeant, Battery A, 879th FA BN. He joined the service on November 5, 1941, and was discharged on October 11, 1945. He was born August 8, 1917, at French Creek. Medals include the Purple Heart, Good Conduct Medal, American Defense Service Medal, European-African-Middle Eastern Service Ribbon with Bronze Arrowhead, and Certificate of Merit.

REX ONEAL CARPENTER: Motor Machinist's Mate Third, was born October 2, 1923, at French Creek. He joined the service on August 2, 1943. Medals include: Philippine Liberation Ribbon, Pacific Theater Ribbon, Victory Medal, and American Theater Ribbon. He was discharged on March 22, 1946.

Rex O. Carpenter

VERNON E. CARPENTER: Sergeant, U.S. Army. He enlisted on February 2, 1948. He served with the Twenty-fifth Infantry Division, 27th Inf., Second Bn. and F. Company. He was stationed in Osaka, Japan, and served in combat in Korea. He received the following: Combat Infantry Badge, Army Good Conduct Medal, Bronze Star with three Oak Leaf Clusters, Korean Service Medal, Silver Star, and honorable discharge.

Vernon E. Carpenter

Donald R. Carr

DONALD RAY CARR: E-4, was born August 2, 1947, in Masontown, Pennsylvania. He resided in Rock Cave at the time of entry. He joined the service on January 18, 1968. He was discharged on January 17, 1974. He received the National Defense Service Medal and was an expert with the M-14 rifle.

Gary L. Carr

GARY LEE CARR: E-4 (T), was born on January 9, 1947, at Buckhannon. He entered the service April 19, 1967, and was discharged on April 20, 1970. Medals include: Marksman with M-14 rifle.

ROBERT L. CARR: E-5, U.S. Army. He was born September 24, 1944, at Hall. He entered the service on August 18, 1965, and was discharged on August 17, 1971. Awards included: National Defense Service Medal, Good Conduct Medal, and Certificate of Achievement.

Robert L. Carr

ROY C. CARR: E-5, U.S. Army. He was drafted on October 25, 1966, and was discharged on October 24, 1968. His address is Rt. 4, Box 502-A, Buckhannon. He received a Sharpshooter Badge, Good Conduct Medal, and Vietnam Liberation Medal.

Roy C. Carr

Archie N. Casto

ARCHIE NEIL CASTO: E-3, U.S. Army, was born June 15, 1940, at French Creek. He was inducted on November 18, 1965, and was discharged on November 17, 1969. He was a rifle expert while serving.

Arnold W. Casto

ARNOLD W. CASTO: Corporal, was born April 13, 1919, at Sago. He joined the service on April 22, 1941, and was discharged on September 26, 1945. He received the Asiatic-Pacific Campaign Ribbon with Bronze Star, the American Defense Service Ribbon, and Good Conduct Medal.

CARL EDWARD CASTO: T/5, U.S. Army, was born June 18, 1919. He entered the service on April 22, 1941. He was awarded three Battle Stars.

DARRELD KEITH CASTO: Sergeant, U.S. Marine Corps, was born August 17, 1934, at French Creek. He entered the service on May 5, 1957, and was discharged on May 5, 1961. While serving he received the National Defense Service Merit, United Nations Medal, Korean Service Medal, and Good Conduct Medal.

Darreld Keith Casto

DONALD JUNIOR CASTO: Sergeant First Class, U.S. Navy, was born April 10, 1922. He entered the service on September 28, 1942. While serving he was awarded four Battle Stars and the Philippine Liberation Ribbon.

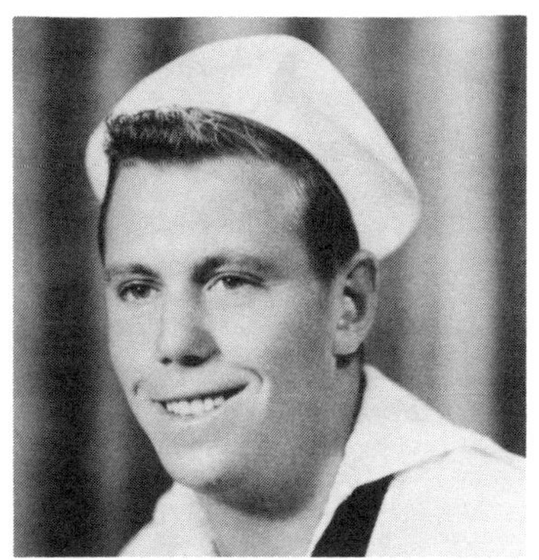

Donald J. Casto

Donald S. Casto

DONALD SCOTT CASTO: E-5, U.S. Navy. He was born October 12, 1948, in Buckhannon. He joined April 9, 1968. He received the National Defense Service Medal, Good Conduct Award—First Award (certificate issued).

Esker D. Casto

ESKER D. CASTO: Basic Airman, regular Air Force. He was discharged on February 3, 1956. He was born in French Creek to Otis and Ada Casto.

JOHN SAMUEL CASTO: Technical Sergeant, U.S. Army. He was born November 4, 1915. He entered the service on September 15, 1941. He was wounded in action on Saipan on Okinawa. He was awarded the Purple Heart with Oak Leaf Cluster and six Battle Stars.

John S. Casto

NEFF J. CASTO: Tech. 5, 321st Engineer Battalion. He was born February 5, 1908, at French Creek. He was inducted on December 31, 1942. He was a sharpshooter with M-1 rifle. He was awarded World War II Victory Medal TWX WD, Good Conduct Medal, Asiatic-Pacific Campaign Medal with Bronze Arrowhead, Philippine Liberation Ribbon, and American Campaign Medal. He was discharged on November 16, 1945.

This poem is dedicated to the boys who have done their "Hitch in Hell" on the Philippines:

Down on the blue Pacific,
on the road to Manila way,
lies the spoils of Halseys Battle,
in the calm San Pedro Bay.

Down on the tuba-soaked isle of Leyte,
A drink that we found first,
Lies the outcasts of the moonshiners,
and the pride of the Three Twenty First.

We fought the Battle of Catmon
And every Jap was shot,
And battled malaria fever,
the itch and tropical rot.

Now living with the helpful natives,
down in Jaro Zone,
down by the Labiranan River,
ten thousand miles from home.

Nobody gives a damn,
but back home we're not forgotten
because we are soldiers
of Uncle Sam.

Soldiers in foreign service,
earn their measly pay
fighting for the country's millions
for a dollar sixty a day.

Patrol duties at Ormoc,
killing Japs by the score,
never forgetting the scrap on Bataan
Or the fight on Corregidor.

Out in the brush with a bolo,
down in a foxhole with a pick,
doing the work of a mule
And never thinking to kick.

Sweat-drenched in the evening
we sit in our foxholes and dream,
waiting to take a shot at a Jap,
for we love to hear him scream.

Bugs at night keep us hopping,
mosquitoes and spiders galore,
Hell no, we're not convicts,
just soldiers on foreign tour.

Up with the sun in the morning,
growling over powdered eggs,
they chase us out on patrolling,
Yea! for this life of dregs.

And when this mess is over
And all our work is done,
our thoughts will turn to Main Street,
as we lay aside our gun.

There will be an Army transport
Come to this hole someday
To take this gang of fighting men
To San Francisco Bay.

And when we are there in Frisco,
and hear the people yell,
we'll know we're back in Heaven,
for we have done our Hitch in Hell.

Submitted by Cpl. Neff J. Casto to the *Record* (newspaper), Buckhannon.

TERRIE MITCHELL CASTO: E-4, U.S. Army. He was born April 25, 1946, in French Creek. He was inducted on December 9, 1965, and was discharged on December 8, 1971. While serving he received the following: National Defense Service Medal, Bronze Star Medal with "V" Device, Expert (Rifle M-14, Rifle M-16), one Overseas Service Bar, Driver Badge, and Good Conduct Medal.

Terrie M. Casto

Coleman G. Channel

COLEMAN G. CHANNEL: E-4, U.S. Army. He was born December 17, 1934, in Alexander. He entered the service in January of 1960. He received Badge, Sharpshooter and Rifle. He was discharged from the U.S. Army Reserve in July 1963.

Orval S. Channel

ORVAL S. CHANNEL: Corporal (T), U.S. Army. He was born February 12, 1932, in Alexander. He enlisted on September 24, 1952, at Fairmont, WV. While serving he received Korean Service Medal with two Bronze Stars, United Service Medal, National Defense Service Medal, MUC, ROKPUC, and Good Conduct Medal. He was discharged on August 19, 1954.

OSCAR E. CHANNEL: Private, Forty-sixth Infantry. He was born in Upshur County. He enlisted on July 14, 1918. He was honorably discharged on February 15, 1919.

Oscar E. Channel

PAUL LEE CHANNEL: Seaman First Class. He enlisted on October 21, 1942, in Cleveland, Ohio, and was discharged May 12, 1944, from U.S. Naval hospital in San Diego, California. Ratings held: S2C, S1C, V6 and USNR (CB).

Paul Lee Channel

RAY WILLIAM CLARK: Motor Machinist's Mate Third Class (T), USN. He was born February 15, 1913, in Buckhannon. He was inducted on February 18, 1944. While serving he received operation and engagement stars on the Asiatic-Pacific Ribbon for participating in the Bismarck Sea Archipelago Campaign from April 7, 1944, to July 31, 1944, Western New Guinea Operations (Morotai) from September 21, 1944, to October 6, 1944, Leyte, Philippine Campaign, from November 6, 1944, to January 5, 1945, and Lingayen Invasion and Occupation from January 9, 1945, to January 27, 1945.

David R. Coates

DAVID R. COATES, JR.: Lieutenant Colonel, U.S. Army. He served more than twenty years in the U.S. Army Signal Corps. He served with the 509th Radio Research Group and the Fourth Transportation Command in the Republic of Vietnam as Signal Officer from July 1968 to December 1969. He was awarded the Bronze Star, Meritorious Service Medal, Joint Service Commendation, and Army Commendation Medal. He was commander of VFW Post 3663 in Buckhannon, 1986-1987.

JOHN COCHERAN: Private First Class, in the U.S. Army. He was born January 5, 1909, in Checkaska, Oklahoma. He joined the service on October 23, 1942 and was discharged on October 1, 1945. He was a sharpshooter and received a Good Conduct Medal.

John Cocheran

JAMES W. COCKERILL: First Sergeant, (E-8), retired. He enlisted on August 6, 1942, in the U.S. Army. He was discharged on December 14, 1945, with being promoted to SSG. He was awarded the Bronze Star Medal for Heroism, the Purple Heart Medal for wounds suffered in action along with numerous other medals and awards. He was in the Army Reserve from December 15, 1945, to September 16, 1947. He went back on active duty on October 15, 1961. Cockerill was discharged again on September 16, 1966. He re-enlisted on August 14, 1971. He was awarded the West Virginia Meritorious Service Medal for recruiting excellence in 1975. He received several medals while serving including: Bronze Star Medal, Good Conduct Medal, American Campaign Medal, Asiatic-Pacific Medal with Bronze Arrowhead, two Bronze Service Stars, World War II Victory Medal, Combat Infantry Badge, Army Commendation Medal, Army Reserve Medal with 20-year clasp, five National Guard Ribbons (one with three Service Stars), National Guard Ribbon with Eagle and three National Guard Unit Citation Awards. He retired on the twenty-first day of October 1980.

James W. Cockerill

LONNIE JOSEPH COLLINS: E-4, U.S. Army. He was born August 10, 1946, in Buckhannon. He was inducted on Octo-

Left to right: Luther and Lonnie Collins, brothers.

ber 25, 1966, and discharged on October 24, 1972. He received the National Defense Service Medal, Vietnam Service Medal, Vietnam Campaign Medal, and Good Conduct Medal.

LUTHER HENRY COLLINS: E-4, U.S. Army. He was born June 30, 1949, in Buckhannon. He was inducted on August 13, 1969, and discharged on August 11, 1975. While serving he received the National Defense Service Medal, Vietnam Service Medal, Republic of Vietnam Campaign Medal and one Overseas Bar.

Roy E. Collins

ROY EDWARD COLLINS: E-5, U.S. Navy. He was born October 12, 1944, in Pickens. He entered the service on February 11, 1966, and was discharged from duty on November 11, 1971. He received the National Defense Service Medal, Navy Unit Commendation, Vietnam Service Medal with four Insignia, Republic of Vietnam Campaign Medal, Combat Action Ribbon, Bronze Stars and Fleet Marine Force Combat Operations.

CHARLES WILLIAM COMBS: Mailman 3/c, SA, U.S. Navy. He was born June 21, 1925, at French Creek. He was inducted on December 11, 1943. He received the American Theater Ribbon and the Victory Medal. He was discharged on March 4, 1946. He re-enlisted again on October 2, 1950, and was honorably dis-

Charles W. Combs

charged on August 26, 1953, as Teleman M 3rd Class, U.S. Naval Reserve.

ROBERT C. COMBS: Technical Sergeant, Thirty-seventh Infantry Division, U.S. Army. He was born May 11, 1923 at Frenchton. He entered the service on March 8, 1944, and was discharged on April 20, 1946. While serving he received the American Theater Ribbon, Asiatic-Pacific Theater Ribbon with one Bronze Star, Philippine Liberation Ribbon with one Bronze Star, Good Conduct Medal, and Victory Medal WW II.

Robert C. Combs

Willis D. Craven

WILLIS D. CRAVEN: Staff Sergeant, U.S. Army. He was born December 6, 1920, in Tallmansville. He entered the service on August 6, 1942, and was honorably discharged on December 15, 1945. He served in Northern France, Ardennes, Rhineland and Central Europe. He was awarded the Good Conduct Medal, Bronze Star Medal, American Theater Ribbon, European-African-Middle Eastern Ribbon and the World War II Victory Ribbon.

William R. Curry

WILLIAM R. CURRY: Sergeant, U.S. Army, Company I, 201st Infantry. He was born October 21, 1915, in Sutton. He was inducted on May 13, 1941, and was discharged on October 3, 1945. He served in the Aleutian Islands. While serving he was awarded the Good Conduct Medal, American Defense Service Medal with one Bronze Service Star, APTO Medal with one Bronze Service Star and the ATO Medal.

WILMER ("DARCY") CUTRIGHT: Private First Class, U.S. Army. In service during the Korean War. He took training at Hawaii Infantry Training Center and served with the 278th Infantry RCT, Company D, Camp Drum, New York, and Company M, Iceland Defense Force.

Wilmer Cutright

TERRY MICHAEL DAFT: E-5, Sergeant, U.S. Marine Corps. He was born January 17, 1947, in Buckhannon. He joined the service on May 3, 1966. He was discharged on February 14, 1972. He received the following awards: National Defense Service Medal, Vietnam Campaign Medal with device, Presidential Unit Citation, Navy Unit Citation, Rifle Marksmanship Badge, Vietnam Service Medal with two stars, Combat Action Ribbon, and Good Conduct Medal.

Terry M. Daft

Edwin C. DeBarr

EDWIN C. DeBARR: PhM/2C, U.S. Navy. He was born on October 12, 1924. He entered the service on July 26, 1943. He served in the U.S. Navy Armed Guard in South, Central and North Pacific. He was awarded three Battle Stars and Commendation from the Secretary of the Navy.

Orville C. DeBarr

ORVILLE CURTIS DeBARR: Private, Company H, Device Battalion Number 2, U.S. Army. Enlisted May 22, 1918 in Buckhannon. He was born February 22, 1895. He was discharged on August 29, 1918, due to old injury to left wrist. He was discharged from Camp Custer, Michigan.

WILBERT L. DeBARR: Corporal, U.S. Army. He was born on June 11, 1920. He entered the service on July 22, 1945, at Shepherd Field, Texas. He served in France, Belgium, and Germany.

Wilbert L. DeBarr

JAMES A. DETAMORE: Technical Sergeant, Company F, 317th Infantry. He was born November 3, 1919, at Flatwoods. He enlisted in the army on May 23, 1939. Participated in Carolina maneuvers in 1941. He had desert training late 1943 and completed that course in April 1944. He sailed from New York Harbor on July 1, 1944, en route to Glasgow, Scotland (arriving July 7, 1944). The Eightieth Division was assigned to General G. S. Patton's Third Army and remained so throughout the war. He fought in the Battle of the Bulge. He was discharged on August 9, 1945. He returned to active duty through the Army Reserve program on July 15, 1948, and was assigned to the U.S. Army Hospital, Camp Pickett, Virginia.

He was transferred to the U.S. Army Hospital, Fort Lee, Virginia, in 1949 when Camp Pickett closed. Camp Pickett reopened as a training center in 1950. He left for Osaka, Japan, in July 1951. He was processed at Camp Drake and was sent to Pusan, Korea, arriving on September 5, 1951. He was placed on field duty in Taegu, Korea, on September 8, 1951, and remained throughout the war. He arrived in the States on May 27, 1953. He was sent to the Sixty-seventh Medical Depot at Einsiedlerhof, Germany, where he arrived in April 1956. He returned to the U.S. Army Dispensary, Fort Hayes, in Columbus, Ohio, in May 1959. He retired from same on August 1, 1962. He was awarded the Purple Heart for wounds received on September 8, 1944, Combat Infantry Badge, Oak Leaf Cluster to Purple Heart for wounds received on January 1, 1945, Bronze Star, and Good Conduct Medal. After army retirement he worked for Federal Civil Service until December 31, 1975. At the completion of this service he was awarded the Distinguished Career Award by the Defense Supply Agency.

James A. Detamore

JOHN L. DETAMORE: Ship's Cook Third Class (T), U.S. Navy. He was born on May 9, 1924, at Centralia. He entered the service on June 21, 1943, and was discharged on December 17, 1945. While serving he received Naval Reserve Medal, Armed Forces Reserve Medal, American Campaign Medal, Asiatic-Pacific Campaign Medal with one silver and two Bronze Stars, World War II Victory Medal, National Defense Service Medal, and Philippine Liberation Ribbon.

Dayle P. Douglas

DAYLE P. DOUGLAS: Colonel, Forty-seventh Regiment, Ninth Infantry Division, U.S. Army. He entered the service on May 13, 1942, and was discharged on May 18, 1945. He received wounds in France on July 4 and August 10, 1944. While serving he received ETO Theater Ribbon with five Bronze Stars, Good Conduct Medal, Purple Heart with Cluster, Distinguished Unit Citation and Combat Badge.

ERWIN VENTEN DOUGLAS: Sergeant (T), Air Force. He was born on December 4, 1929, at Rock Cave. He entered the service on July 22, 1948, and was discharged on June 4, 1952. While serving he completed a course of military training for mechanics. He also completed a course in special waterproofing conducted by the Troop Training Unit, Amphibious Training Command/Force, U.S. Atlantic Fleet.

Erwin V. Douglas

FRANKLIN C. ELLIS: Lieutenant Commander, U.S. Navy. He joined in July 1943 and retired on March 1, 1969. He served in Normandy.

Franklin C. Ellis

James L. Ellis

JAMES L. ELLIS: U.S. Navy. He served aboard the *Lexington Currier* in 1945. Elected to be an air cadet. Attended Iowa preflight and war ended prior to his receiving commission and wings.

RICHARD LEE ELLIS: Private, U.S. Army. He was born in Gaines City. He was inducted on May 13, 1918. He engaged in the Gerardmer Section Vosges Mountains and Meuse-Argonne Offensive. He left the United States for foreign service on July 6, 1918, and arrived back in the States on July 3, 1919. He was entitled to wear one gold chevron. He was discharged on June 9, 1919.

Bobby R. Fawley

BOBBY RAY FAWLEY: He joined the service in September 1958 and retired on October 3, 1977. He lives at 91 Hickory Flat, Buckhannon. He served in Lebanon, Cuba and Vietnam. While serving he received three Good Conduct Medals, Vietnam Service Award, and Defense Service Award.

RONALD LEE FAWLEY: E-5, U.S. Army (Sergeant T). He was born March 12, 1942, in Elkins. While serving he received the National Defense Service Medal, Vietnam Campaign Medal, Vietnam Service Medal with two Campaign Stars, two Overseas Service Bars, Bronze Star Medal, Expert Badge (M-14), Army Commendation Medal with V Device, Combat Infantryman's Badge, Sharpshooter Badge (M-60), and Marksman Badge (M-16). He was discharged on May 24, 1973.

Ronald Lee Fawley

RONALD L. FENSTERMACHER: Private First Class, was awarded the Purple Heart for wounds received in action in Vietnam on July 24, 1966, resulting in his death. Award was made on August 23, 1966.

Ronald L. Fenstermacher

Hubert H. Fleming

HUBERT H. FLEMING: Private First Class, Headquarters Battery, 315th Field Artillery Battalion. He was born July 17, 1918, in Braxton County. He entered the service on July 23, 1942, and was honorably discharged on November 18, 1946. He served in Northern France, Rhineland, Ardennes and Central Europe. He was awarded the following: Good Conduct Medal, Meritorious Unit Award, European-African-Middle Eastern Service Ribbon, and American Theater Service.

RONALD LEE FOWLER: E-5, U.S. Army. He was born on September 25, 1945, in Clarksburg. He joined the service on September 5, 1968. He was discharged on September 4, 1974. He received numerous badges and ribbons while serving.

William C. Fumerola

WILLIAM CHARLES FUMEROLA: Sergeant, U.S. Army. He was born on June 12, 1930, in Red Rock. He was inducted on November 28, 1951. While serving he received the Combat Infantry Badge, Korean Service Medal with two Bronze Campaign Stars, and United Nation Service Medal.

HARVEY J. GASTON: Technical 5, Battery C, 662nd Field Artillery Battalion, U.S. Army. He was born June 6, 1907, in Buckhannon. He was inducted on April 9, 1944, and was honorably discharged on October 27, 1945. He served in Rhineland and Central Europe. While serving he received the European-African-Middle Eastern Service Ribbon and the Good Conduct Medal.

Harvey J. Gaston.

JOHN F. GASTON: Private, Battery B, 248th Field Artillery. He was discharged in May 1945. He passed away on January 31, 1965. While serving he was awarded the European-African-Middle Eastern Theater Ribbon. He was inducted on July 7, 1942.

John F. Gaston

Ronald L. Gifford

RONALD LEE GIFFORD: Corporal, U.S. Army. He was born July 15, 1945, in Buckhannon. While serving he received the National Defense Service Medal, Vietnam Service Medal with two Stars and Vietnam Campaign Medal with Device.

Thurman L. Gillespie

THURMAN LYNN GILLESPIE: Ship's Cook First Class (T), U.S. Navy. He was born on February 6, 1915, at Palmer. He enlisted on January 29, 1942. He served on numerous vessels while in the service.

JOSEPH S. GOULD: Private First Class, U.S. Army. He served his country from 1942 to 1945. He was with the Twelfth Armored Division of B Company, Seventeenth Armored Infantry Battalion. He was awarded the following medals: American Campaign, World War II Victory Medal, European-African-Middle Eastern Campaigns, Bronze Star, Combat Infantryman, Good Conduct Medal, Purple Heart, and French Decorations.

Joseph S. Gould

GEORGE ARTHUR GROVE: First Lieutenant, U.S. Air Force. He received his wings on March 22, 1953. He enlisted in 1952. He was a jet pilot in Alaska where he went down with his plane off the coast of Anchorage shortly after takeoff on March 30, 1953. Neither his body nor the plane were found.

George A. Grove

Ernest Grubb

ERNEST GRUBB: Technical-5, Infantry. He was inducted on December 28, 1944, and discharged on November 21, 1946. He trained at Camp Hood, Texas, and Camp Maxy, Texas. He received the Asiatic-Pacific Ribbon, Philippine Liberation, Victory Medal, Good Conduct Medal and two Overseas Service Bars. He was honorably discharged.

Joseph M. Guth

JOSEPH M. GUTH: Private First Class, U.S. Army. He was born February 27, 1921, at Buckhannon. He was inducted on October 30, 1942, and was discharged on October 25, 1945. While serving he was awarded the EAME Ribbon with two Stars.

CHARLES C. HALTERMAN: U.S. Army. He served from 1943 to 1945. While serving he was wounded in Germany.

Charles C. Halterman

Clifford L. Halterman

CLIFFORD LAWRENCE HALTERMAN: Fireman First Class (Electrician's Mate), SV 6, U. S. Navy. He was inducted on April 7, 1944, and was discharged on October 15, 1945. He served on the NRS Huntington, WV, USNTS Great Lakes, Illinois, and USS *Ellet* (DD398).

James Halterman

JAMES HALTERMAN: U.S. Army. He was in the Philippine Death March in 1941. He had a career in the service. He died in the Louisiana fire in 1955.

WILLIAM HENRY HALTERMAN: First Lieutenant, U.S. Army. He was born April 16, 1919. He entered the service on January 25, 1941. He served in Iceland, Burma and the Pacific. He was killed in action at Imphal, India, on June 6, 1944. He was awarded the Purple Heart, Bronze Star Medal, and Distinguished Flying Cross.

William H. Halterman

DIXON D. HAMNER: Private First Class, Company H, 188th Parachute Infantry. He was born on November 22, 1923, at French Creek. He was inducted on June 21, 1943, and discharged on January 20, 1946. While serving he received the Asiatic-Pacific Theater Ribbon with three Bronze Stars, the Philippine Liberation Ribbon with one Bronze Service Star, Good Conduct Medal, Distinguished Unit Citation, Bronze Arrowhead and World War II Victory Medal. He was honorably discharged.

Dixon D. Hamner

Joe V. Hamner

JOE V. HAMNER: Private First Class, Company B, 2755th Engineer Combat Battalion. He was born on March 10, 1920, in French Creek. He entered the military on March 28, 1942, and was honorably discharged on September 13, 1945. He received the Good Conduct Medal, European-African-Middle Eastern Service Ribbon with one Bronze Arrowhead, American Theater Service Ribbon, Meritorious Service Unit Insignia with one Gold Star.

LESTER EDWARD HAMRICK: E-6, U.S. Army. He was born October 14, 1934, in Webster Springs. He joined the service at Fort Benning, Georgia. While serving he received a Certificate of Appreciation for duty from April 3, 1951, through

May 31, 1972, Certificate of Appreciation on May 31, 1972, Certificate of Achievement, The Distinguished Flying Cross, Bronze Star Medal, two Air Medals, Commendation Medal for Meritorious achievement in the Republic of Vietnam from March 22, 1970, to July 18, 1970, and July 1967 to July 1968.

James S. Harris

JAMES S. HARRIS: E-7, regular army medical. He joined the service the first time on June 20, 1951, and followed with re-enlistments. He was born May 11, 1934, in Webster Springs. He was awarded numerous medals and commendations: Purple Heart, Combat Medical Badge, Korean Service Medal with two Bronze Service Stars, United Nations Service Medal with one Overseas Bar, Good Conduct Medal, National Defense Service Medal, second Good Conduct Medal, Expert M-1 Rifle, SS .45 cal. Pistol, CMB (second award), Vietnam Service Medal, NDSM with OLC, GCM Fifth Award, VCM, VSM, VNCG with BS Development, BSM, BSM with first OLC. He was awarded a Certificate of Achievement from the Thirty-first Medical Group, U.S. Army Europe, for his meritorious performance of duty during the period from July 3, 1966, to February 6, 1969. He received at least three Certificates of Training: one from the 46th Surgical Hospital (MA) for blood banking procedures course, class No. 5, one from Fort Hood, Texas, from the First Armored Division Intelligence School and one for the advanced medical specialist course (911.3). He retired from the army on September 1, 1971.

Lida K. Hawkins

LIDA KEVIN HAWKINS: E-4, U.S. Army. He was born December 14, 1950, at 4 Circle Drive, Buckhannon. He was inducted on August 6, 1970, and discharged August 5, 1976. While serving he received the following medals, badges, etc.: National Defense Service Medal with Combat Infantryman Badge, Vietnam Campaign Medal with 60 Device, Vietnam Cross of Gallantry with Air Medal, Vietnam Service Medal with one Bronze Service Star, Bronze Star Medal, and the Purple Heart.

WILBERT EARL HAWKINS: Private First Class, Company B, 104th Infantry Advanced Training Battalion. He was born on November 1, 1918, and died on April 12, 1982. He enlisted on August 5, 1940, and was discharged on August 23, 1945. He served in the Aleutian Islands and received the following awards: Good Conduct Medal, American Defense Service Medal with one Bronze Star, and the American Pacific Service Ribbon.

Wilbert E. Hawkins

JERL HEATER: Private, U.S. Army. He enlisted in the service in February 1942 and served outside the U.S. for nine months. He served in the litter squadron of the Medical Corps during the African campaign. He was awarded a ribbon for his participation in the Battle for Africa. He was also awarded two chevrons which denotes service on foreign territory. He was a victim of shell shock and was returned to the States and admitted to the hospital in White Sulphur Springs in West Virginia.

Jerl Heater

Martin S. Heater

MARTIN SCOTT HEATER: E-5, U.S. Army. He was born on February 11, 1948, in French Creek. While serving his country he received the Bronze Star, National Defense Service Medal, Vietnam Service Medal, Vietnam Campaign Medal, two Overseas Bars, Expert Badge Rifle (M-14), Expert Badge Rifle (M-16), Drivers Mechanic Badge, and Good Conduct Medal. He was honorably discharged on December 18, 1972.

RICHARD OMAR HEATHERLY: Corporal (T). He was born March 12, 1929, in Buckhannon. He was inducted on February 23, 1951, and discharged on January 30, 1953. He received the Occupation Medal (Germany) while serving his country.

Ray E. Hefner

RAY ERVIN HEFNER: Sergeant First Class (T), U.S. Army. He was born April 23, 1926, in French Creek. He was inducted on November 28, 1951, and discharged on November 19, 1953. While serving he received the Korean Service Medal with two Bronze Stars, United Nations Service Medal, Combat Medic Badge, National Defense Service Medal and Good Conduct Medal. He was a member of Medical Company, 180th Infantry Regiment, Forty-fifth Infantry Division. He now lives in French Creek.

CHARLES RICHARD HELMICK: E-4, U.S. Army. He was born May 21, 1948, in Buckhannon. He was inducted on January 28, 1969, and was discharged on January 27, 1975. He received the National Defense Service Medal, Vietnam Medal with 60 Device, Expert (M-16), Vietnam Service Medal with two Overseas Service Bar, Army Commendation Medal, and Marksman (M-14).

Charles R. Helmick

CHARLES V. HELMICK: Private First Class, U.S. Army. He was born May 22, 1927, in French Creek. He enlisted on December 3, 1945, and was discharged on May 24, 1947. While serving he was awarded the Victory Medal.

Charles V. Helmick

Arthur H. Hiner

ARTHUR H. HINER: Sergeant, Service Battery, 805th Field Artillery Battalion, U.S. Army. He was born June 20, 1914, at Sand Run, Buckhannon. He was inducted on November 13, 1941. He was discharged October 17, 1945. He served in Northern France and Rhineland. He received the Good Conduct Medal, American Defense Service Medal, and the European-African-Middle Eastern Service Ribbon.

J. D. HINKLE, JR.: Tech., Fourth Grade, Seventy-sixth Station Hospital. He enlisted on October 6, 1942, entered active duty on May 1, 1943, and was honorably discharged on January 18, 1949. He was an X-ray technician 864. He was awarded the following medals, etc.: Asiatic-Pacific Theater with one Bronze Service Star, Philippine Liberation with two Bronze Service Stars, Good Conduct Medal, and World War II Victory Medal.

Retice J. Hinkle

RETICE J. HINKLE: Private First Class 35391252, 192nd General Hospital, U.S. Army, was returned to the United States on the ship HMS *Queen Elizabeth* which sailed from Southampton, England, on August 26, 1945.

VALENTINE C. HINKLE, JR.: Private First Class, Company C, 1268th Engineer C Battalion. He was born April 15, 1920, at Alexander. He was inducted on February 1, 1945, and was discharged on August 3, 1946. He was awarded the Good Conduct Medal, Asiatic-Pacific Service Medal, World War II Victory Medal and Occupation Ribbon while serving his country.

Valentine C. Hinkle

William Z. Hinkle

WILLIAM Z. HINKLE: Private, U.S. Army. He was born in Alexander. He was inducted into the service on November 30, 1942, and was honorably discharged on November 12, 1943.

JUDSON J. HODGES: Captain, 1106th AAF Unit, U.S. Army. He was born on October 17, 1923, in Buckhannon. He joined the Army on July 11, 1941, and was honorably discharged on November 12, 1942. While serving he received the following medals: Victory Medal, European-African-Middle Eastern Service Medal, and American Service Medal.

CHARLES L. HORNBECK: First Sergeant, U.S. Army, Company C, 116th Medical Battalion. He was born in Upshur County. He was wounded in New Guinea on August 2, 1943. He served in Southern Philippines, Papua and New Guinea. He was inducted on March 28, 1942, and was honorably discharged on September 12, 1945. While serving he received the Asiatic-Pacific Theater Ribbon with three Bronze Stars, Philippine Liberation Ribbon with one Bronze Star, Good Conduct Ribbon, and Purple Heart. He also received the Silver Star and the Bronze Star in 1978 for duty as a Combat Medic.

DUFFY C. HORNBECK, JR.: Staff Sergeant, U.S. Army. He was born July 8, 1925, in Buckhannon. He was inducted on September 27, 1943, and went into active duty on November 16, 1943, and was discharged on the twenty-first of November, 1945. He was in the Ardennes, Rhineland and Central European Campaigns for which he was awarded three Bronze Stars and an Air Medal.

Duffy C. Hornbeck, Jr.

Billy Joe House

BILLY JOE HOUSE: Staff Sergeant, U.S. Army, HHC, 240th Quartermaster Battalion. He was born June 9, 1928, in Buckhannon. He retired after serving his country for twenty-six years and twenty-two days. He was awarded the Army Occupation Medal (Germany), Good Conduct Medal with Second Award, Combat Infantry Badge, Korean Service Medal with five Bronze Stars, American Defense Medal, National Defense Service Medal with one Oak Leaf Cluster, Vietnam Service Medal with five Bronze Stars, Vietnam Campaign Medal with Device in 1960, Republic of Vietnam Cross of Gallantry with Palm, Bronze Star Medal, and Army Commendation Medal.

MYRON BERNARD HYMES: World War I Veteran. He enlisted in the spring of 1918. He was accepted as Second Lieutenant, Infantry, USA, September 16, 1918, served with SATC, Fort Sheridan, Illinois, and Infantry Replacement and Training Troops, Camp Grant, Illinois. He was honorably discharged per S. O. 333, par. 46, Hq., Camp Grant, Illinois, on December 2, 1918.

Myron B. Hymes

JOHN M. HYRE: Sergeant, U.S. Army, Company C, 202nd Engineer C Battalion. He was born September 21, 1923, at French Creek. He was inducted on February 25, 1943, and was honorably discharged on November 27, 1945. While serving he received the Good Conduct Medal, American Theater Service Ribbon, European-African-Middle Eastern Service Ribbon, and World War II Victory Ribbon.

John M. Hyre

MARY MABLE HYRE: Pharmacist's Mate Third Class, U.S. Navy. She was born May 13, 1917, at French Creek. She enlisted on March 23, 1944, and was honorably discharged on January 7, 1947.

Zola and Mary Hyre

ZOLA HYRE: Pharmacist's Mate Third Class, U.S. Navy. She was born on September 19, 1919, at French Creek. She entered active duty on March 7, 1944. She was entitled to American Theater and Victory Ribbons for her participation in World War II.

RALPH R. HYRE: Private First Class, Battery A, 903rd Field Artillery Battalion. He was born December 1, 1922, at Rock Cave. He was inducted on January 26, 1944, and went into active duty on February 16, 1944. He was discharged on April 24, 1946. While serving he was awarded the Good Conduct Medal, European-African-Middle Eastern Theater Ribbon, World War II Victory Ribbon, and Army Occupation Medal (Germany).

EDWARD J. IRELAND: U.S. Navy. He went into the service on May 20, 1943, and returned after the war was over in February 1946. He served on the USS *Montpelier* (CL-57). He was a Search Radar Operator and later a Fire Control Director. The *Montpelier* was the Flagship for the American Victory on November 2, 1943, in the Battle of Empress Augusta Bay. The *Montpelier* also saw action in the Central Solomons, Bismarcks, the Invasion of Borneo and the East China Sea. She was later transferred to the Atlantic Fleet.

NATHANIEL JACK: Sergeant, Service Training, 112th Cavalry Regiment, U.S. Army. He was born on November 16, 1918, in Buckhannon. He was inducted on July 3, 1941, and was honorably discharged on August 20, 1945. While serving he was awarded the following medals, etc.: Asiatic-Pacific Theater Ribbon with four Bronze Stars per WD GO #33/45, American Defense Service Medal, Philippine Liberation Ribbon with one Bronze Star per WD GO #33/45 and Good Conduct Ribbon per GO 1 Hq 112th Cav. on February 10, 1944. He was a member of the Fighting Texans troop of the U.S. Sixth Army which gave the Allies its Arawe hold on the New Britain Islands. He had served in the South Pacific theater of operations for almost three years. A small American commando force, paddling toward shore in rubber boats in the moonlight, was subjected to a merciless barrage of machine-gun and cannon fire from ashore, spearheaded by amphibious tanks and wrested the entire Arawe Peninsula from the Japanese. From an escort destroyer he saw the Japanese tracers stream in among the commando rubber boats. He heard the thump-thump of the small rapid-fire Japanese cannon interspersed with the rattle of machine guns. Then with the aid of field glasses and the moonlight, he picked out the figures of heavily armed men struggling in the water, rubber boats empty and drifting, other boats with their occupants paddling furiously with the tracers streaking all around them and cannon shells tossing up geysers of spray. Private Jack was awarded the Good Conduct Medal for exemplary behavior, efficiency and fidelity. This report was given by an eyewitness of the United Press.

Nathaniel Jack

STANLEY JESKIE: Sergeant First Class, U.S. Army. He entered the service on November 8, 1940. He died while still in the service on December 25, 1959. While serving he received the American Defense Service Ribbon with one Bronze Star, American Theater Ribbon, and Good Conduct Medal. He served in Korea.

Charles J. Johnson

CHARLES J. JOHNSON: Corporal, 66th Air Service Squadron, U.S. Army. He was born on December 31, 1911, at Lorentz. He enlisted in the service on August 26, 1942, and was honorably discharged on January 2, 1946. While serving he was awarded the Asiatic-Pacific Theater Ribbon with three Bronze Stars, Philippine Liberation Ribbon with one Bronze Star, Good Conduct Medal and Victory Medal World War II.

ELLIOT M. KARICKHOFF: 1697 Labor Supply Company. Served in Normandy, Southern France, and Central Europe. Joined the service on March 28, 1942, and was discharged on November 5, 1945. He was awarded the African-Middle Eastern Ribbon with three Bronze Stars, Good Conduct Medal, American Theater Ribbon, and World War II Victory Medal.

LINDON L. KERNS: Staff Sergeant, Company F, 317th Infantry Regiment, U.S. Army. He was born October 24, 1921, in Margaret. He was inducted on July 6, 1942, and honorably discharged on September 25, 1945. While serving he was awarded the Purple Heart for wounds received on September 8, 1944, the Combat Infantry Badge on September 23, 1944, the Oak Leaf Cluster to the Purple Heart for wounds received on January 1, 1945, the Bronze Star and Good Conduct Medal. Cam-

Lindon L. Kerns

paigns: American Defense Medal, European-African-Middle Eastern Service Medal, American Campaign Medal, World War II Victory Medal, Army of Occupation Medal, National Defense Medal, Korean Service Medal, and United Nations Service Medal for Korea.

RONALD LEE KESLING: Corporal, U.S. Marine Corps. He was born March 4, 1947, in Buckhannon. He enlisted in the service on July 22, 1966. He was awarded the Military Merit Medal, Gallantry Cross with Palm, Engraved Purple Heart, three medals, two Gold Star Lapel buttons, National Defense Service Medal, Vietnam Service Medal, and Republic of Vietnam Campaign Medal. He was killed in action in the vicinity of Thua Thien and Quangtri provinces, Vietnam. He was killed on the twenty-seventh of December, 1967.

Ronald L. Kesling

MORRIS R. KIDDY: 192 Airport Street, Keyser. He joined the service on August 6, 1952, and was discharged on May 7, 1954. He received the Combat Medical Badge, Korean Service Medal with two Battle Stars, and Good Conduct Medal.

FRANCIS BACEL KITTLE: Seaman First Class, U.S. Navy. He was honorably discharged on December 17, 1945.

James C. Kittle

JAMES C. KITTLE: Private, 1060th Army Air Forces Base Unit (Aviation Engineers). He enlisted on July 28, 1945, and was discharged on July 9, 1946. He received the Army of Occupation Medal World War II with Germany Clasp and World War II Victory Medal.

HAROLD RAY KOON, JR.: Staff Sergeant, U.S. Air Force. He was born July 12, 1931, at Tenmile. He entered the service on February 12, 1951, as an air corps cadet. He was killed when his C-47 transport apparently developed engine trouble after takeoff from the Tainan Air Force Base. Sergeant Koon attended the Air Technical School at Keesler Field, Mississippi, where he graduated as a radio operator in 1952. He served in the Korean War and several other countries. He lost his life on November 6, 1959, in Southern Formosa.

Harold R. Koon, Jr.

LEON K. LAWSON: Private First Class, U.S. Marine Corps. He was born November 21, 1893, at Auburn. He enlisted for service on July 28, 1917. He served with American Expeditionary Forces in Europe from February 25, 1918, until July 17, 1919. He was wounded in Soissons Sector on July 18, 1919. He served in Chateau-Thierry Sector (Belleau Woods), Soissons Sector (Vierzy), Champagne Sector (Battle of Mount "Blanc Mont") and Meuse-Argonne Sector. He also participated in the march to Rhine River for occupation of Coblenz Bridgehead, Germany, Army of Occupation, Germany, and was recommended for re-enlistment and a Good Conduct Medal.

Leon K. Lawson

Stephen T. Lesondak

STEPHEN THOMAS LESONDAK: Aviation Machinist's Mate Second Class, U.S. Navy. He was born September 1910 in Marguerite, Pennsylvania. He was in active duty from September 14, 1942, to September 23, 1945, when he was honorably discharged. He served on the USNRS Pittsburgh, Pennsylvania, NTS NOB Norfolk, Virginia, Patrol Wing 5 Hedron, Fleet Air Wing 15 Hedron, Patrol Squadron 73, Hedron 9-1, Fleet Air Wing 9, Hedron FAW 12, USNH Key West Florida, Patrol Bombing Squadron #204, NYd Philadelphia, Pennsylvania, CASU #26, and USN Personnel Separation Center, Boston, Massachusetts.

Stephen T. Lesondak, Jr.

STEPHEN THOMAS LESONDAK, JR.: E-4, U.S. Army. He was born on April 24, 1947, in Buckhannon. He was inducted on October 25, 1968, and was honorably discharged on October 24, 1972. He was awarded the NDS Medal, Good Conduct Medal, and Expert (M-14).

CARL R. LEWIS: He joined the U.S. Navy on June 15, 1917, for a four-year term and served as a pharmacist attached to the U.S. Marine Corps. He served in France and Germany during World War I. He was honorably discharged from the navy on August 22, 1919. He was a bricklayer and stonemason by trade. He was a lifetime member of VFW Post 3663. He died January 8, 1973.

Carl R. Lewis

DANA THRELL LEWIS: Motor Machinist's Mate Second Class, U.S. Navy. He was born July 15, 1917, at Rock Cave. He was inducted on October 12, 1943, and was honorably discharged on December 20, 1945. He won the following medals: American Area, Victory World War II, Asiatic Pacific Area and Philippine Liberation.

Dana T. Lewis

P. D. Lewis

P. D. (JACK) LEWIS: Technical Sergeant, U.S. Army. He was born March 1, 1918, in Buckhannon. He enlisted on July 1, 1940, and was honorably discharged on August 23, 1945. While serving he received the Good Conduct Medal, American Defense Service Medal with one Bronze Star, and Asiatic-Pacific Service Ribbon.

Lejeune Lewis

LEJEUNE LEWIS: USNR Gunner's Mate Third Class. Ratings held: AS, S2/c, S1/c and GM3/c. He entered the service on June 30, 1943, and was honorably discharged on March 12, 1946. He did twenty-five months of sea duty in the Atlantic and Pacific. He was awarded the following awards: European Theater Ribbon, Pacific Theater Ribbon, American Theater Ribbon, and the Victory Medal.

PERRY C. LEWIS: U.S. Marine Corps. He joined the service on January 31, 1942, and was honorably discharged on January 30, 1946. He received his combat training at the Marine Depot in San Diego, California, and was attached to the Signal Corps and actively participated in combat against the Japanese on Guadalcanal (Solomon Islands), Tarawa (Gilbert Islands), Saipan and Tinian (Mariana Islands). He practiced combat training on Maui, Hononlulu, and Hilo, Hawaii. He served in Efate, New Hebrides, Eniwetok, Marshall Islands, Noumea, New Caledonia, Auckland, Wellington, and New Zealand. He has been a member of VFW Post 3663 since 1946. He received three Campaign Ribbons, Presidential Award, Asiatic-Pacific Award, Good Conduct Award and four Combat Stars. He is a jeweler, watch and jewelry repairman. He also designed and built the Lewis Building in Buckhannon.

Perry C. Lewis

JAMES G. LINGER: Corporal, U.S. Army. He was born October 12, 1923, at French Creek. He was inducted on February 27, 1943, and honorably discharged on October 17, 1945. While serving he received the following medals: Good Conduct Medal, Distinguished Unit Badge with one Oak Leaf Cluster and European-African-Middle Eastern Service Medal with eight Bronze Stars. He served in Naples-Foggia, Rome-Arno, Northern France, Southern France, Rhineland, Northern Apennines, Po Valley and Air Offensive, Balkans.

WILLIAM J. LINGER: Technical 4, Headquarters Company, First Battalion, 343rd Infantry, Eighty-sixth Division, U.S. Army. He was born July 2, 1922, in Weston. He was inducted on February 5, 1943, and was honorably discharged on March 10, 1946. He served in Central Europe. While serving he received the following: European-African-Middle Eastern Theater Ribbon with one Bronze Star, Asiatic Pacific Theater Ribbon, Good Conduct Medal, and the Victory Medal.

William J. Linger

Clifford D. Loudin

CLIFFORD DAVID LOUDIN: Sergeant (T), U.S. Army. He was born on October 21, 1931, in Buckhannon. He enlisted on February 7, 1952, and was honorably discharged on February 7, 1956. While serving he received the Good Conduct Medal, Korean Service Medal with two Bronze Stars, United Nations Service Medal, Combat Infantry Badge, and National Defense Service Medal.

CLIFFORD DAVID LOUDIN, JR.: E-5, U.S. Marines. He was born December 13, 1957. He went into the service on November 20, 1975. While serving he was awarded the Rifle Expert Badge (Second Award), Meritorious Mast (two), and Good Conduct Medal.

Clifford D. Loudin, Jr.

GEORGE OWEN LOUDIN: Seaman First Class. He was born December 20, 1919, in French Creek. He was honorably discharged from the U.S. Navy on November 26, 1945, from Bainbridge, Maryland. Died October 11, 1984.

George O. Loudin

John O. Loudin

JOHN O. LOUDIN: Private First Class, U.S. Army. He was born December 20, 1919, in French Creek. He was honorably discharged on October 3, 1945, from Fort George G. Meade, Maryland. He served in Tunisia, Sicily, Normandy, Northern France, Rhineland, Ardennes and Central Europe. While serving he received the following medals: Good Conduct Medal, American Defense Service Medal, and European-African-Middle Eastern Service Ribbon.

William H. Loudin

WILLIAM HOWARD LOUDIN: Staff Sergeant, U.S. Army, Company A, Third Michigan Battalion, USAINSCOMAS. Observation airplane repairer, 15 years and four months; administrative specialist seven years and two months. He was born September 5, 1945, at Evergreen. He was honorably retired on February 28, 1986. He received the following awards, medals, etc., while serving: Army Commendation Medal, Army Achievement Medal with one Oak Leaf Cluster, Good Conduct Medal (sixth award), National Defense Service Medal, Vietnam Service Medal (eight campaigns), NCO Professional Development Ribbon (3), Army Service Ribbon, Overseas Service Ribbon, Republic of Vietnam Campaign Medal, Republic of Vietnam Gallantry Cross, Unit Citation Badge with Palm, Aircraft Crewman Badge (Senior), M-16 Rifle (Sharpshooter).

GEORGE C. LOUGH: Private First Class, U.S. Army, 626th Medical Clearing Company. He was born September 3, 1922, at Linn. He was inducted on December 28, 1942, and honorably discharged on February 21, 1946. He served in Ardennes, Rhineland and Central Europe. While serving he received the Good Conduct Medal, American Theater Ribbon, European-African-Middle Eastern Theater Ribbon, and World War II Victory Ribbon.

George C. Lough

LONIE R. LOWE: Private, U.S. Army. He was born in Buckhannon. He was inducted on September 3, 1918. He served in Company L, Third Battalion Infantry Replacement and Training Camp, Camp Lee, Virginia, Prov. Company September Auto. Replacement Draft, Company M, 161st Infantry and Fifth Company, Second Training Battalion, 154th Depot Brigade. He was honorably discharged on March 11, 1919. He was born November 16, 1896, and died January 9, 1961.

Lonie R. Lowe

Howard D. Lynch

HOWARD D. LYNCH: Technical Fourth Grade, 4605th Quartermaster Truck Company, U.S. Army, was honorably discharged on November 1, 1946.

William F. McClain

WILLIAM F. McCLAIN: Technical 5, U.S. Army. He was born May 22, 1926, in Buckhannon. He was inducted on September 30, 1944, and was discharged on Nov. 25, 1946. While serving he received the Asiatic-Pacific Service Medal, Good Conduct Medal and World War II Victory Medal.

GARY LEE McCORD: E-5, U.S. Air Force. He was born October 23, 1943, at Tallmansville. He went into the service on June 6, 1966, and was discharged on March 8, 1972. He was awarded the NDSM, AFOUA, AFEM, and AFGCM while serving.

JUNIOR O. MACKEY: Private First Class, U.S. Army. He was born May 9, 1919, in Buckhannon. He was inducted on April 9, 1944, and was honorably discharged on January 7, 1946. While serving he did duty in Rhineland and Central Europe. He was awarded the following: Good Conduct Medal, Purple Heart Medal, Bronze Star Medal, World War II Victory Ribbon, European-African-Middle Eastern Theater Ribbon.

Junior O. Mackey

PAUL B. MACKEY: Technical 5, U.S. Army. He was born January 29, 1922, in Buckhannon. He saw duty in New Guinea and South Philippines. While serving he received the Philippine Liberation Ribbon, Good Conduct Medal, World War II Victory Medal and Asiatic-Pacific Theater Ribbon with two Bronze Service Stars. He was honorably discharged on December 5, 1945.

Paul B. Mackey

Charles F. McLain

CHARLES F. (JOE) McLAIN: U.S. Navy. He enlisted in June 1952 and was discharged in August 1971. He was stationed at Naval Training Center, San Diego, California, Naval Storekeepers School, Newport, Rhode Island, Naval Base, Norfolk, Virginia, Submarine School, New London, Connecticut, Naval Base, Danang, Vietnam. He sailed on the USS ships: *Onslow, Raymond, Turner, Henley, Tidewater, Brumley, Samuel Gompers, Piedmont.* He was awarded the following: National Defense Service Medal, Vietnam Service Medal, Navy Unit Commendation Ribbon, and Republic of Vietnam Campaign Medal.

Anthony Marino

ANTHONY (TONY) MARINO: U.S. Navy, First Class Machinist's Mate. He served his country from 1943 to 1947 through amphibious landing forces. He served in North African and European Operations Theater. He was honorably discharged.

C. WOODFORD MARSH: 877th Air Engineer Squadron, Radar Operator. He entered the service on March 28, 1942, and was discharged on October 21, 1945. He was a sharpshooter with .03 rifle. He served in Tunisia, Sicily, Naples-Foggia, Rome-Arno, North Apennines, Rhineland, Central Europe, and North Africa. He was awarded the European-African-Middle Eastern Service Ribbon and the Good Conduct Medal. He passed away on May 9, 1987.

HOMER HARDING MARTIN: U.S. Navy, Aviation Machinist's Mate First Class. He was born December 7, 1920, at French Creek. He enlisted July 8, 1942, and was honorably discharged November 13, 1945. He served on NOB Norfolk, VA, SSq 69, MAS Kaneohe TH, CASS 36, USS SAIDOR CVE-7, Fighting Squad 41 and Fighting Squad 37.

EDWIN H. MEARNS: Private First Class, U.S. Army. He was born September 7, 1923, at Rock Cave. He was inducted on August 16, 1943, and honorably discharged on March 25, 1946. He served in Central Europe. He was awarded the American Theater Ribbon, Eame Theater Ribbon with one Bronze Star, Asiatic-Pacific Theater Ribbon, Good Conduct Medal, and World War II Victory Medal.

Edwin H. Mearns

RALPH W. MEARNS: Corporal, Regular Army, was honorably discharged on March 24, 1948. He was born January 10, 1928, in Rock Cave. He enlisted September 27, 1946. While serving he received the World War II Victory Medal and the Occupation Meda MTO.

CARL DAVID MELTON: Chief Construction Electrician, U.S. Navy. He was born June 14, 1939, in Upshur County. He expired on July 11, 1986, in Tampa, Florida. He served his country for twenty-six years before being transferred to the Fleet Reserve. While serving he received seven Good Conduct Medals, Navy Unit Citation, Republic of Vietnam Armed with Gallantry Cross, two Meritorious Unit Commendations, two Navy Unit Commendations, National Defense Service Medal, Vietnam Service Medal, Vietnam Campaign Medal, Anartic Service Medal, Navy Expeditionary Medal, two Sea Service Ribbons, Battle "E" Award, and the Vietnam Civic Action Award.

Victor E. Mick

VICTOR EARL MICK: Private, U.S. Army, Company C, 103rd Machine Gun Battalion. He was born in Upshur County. He entered the service on June 5, 1917, and was discharged on April 30, 1919. He served in France from October 2, 1918, to April 17, 1919. He was awarded Service Stripes.

RALPH H. MILES: Technical 5, U.S. Army. He was born July 5, 1924, at Lorentz. He was inducted on March 31, 1944, and was discharged on May 19, 1946. He served in Rhineland and Central Europe. While serving he was awarded the following: Good Conduct Medal, European-African-Middle Eastern Theater Ribbon, and World War II Victory Ribbon.

KALE M. MILLS: Private First Class, U.S. Army. He was born June 1, 1917, at Kedron. He was inducted on February 18, 1942, and was honorably discharged on September 27, 1945. He served in Naples-Foggia, Rome-Arno, Rhineland, North Apennines and Po Valley. He received the following medals, etc.: Good Conduct Medal and the European-African-Middle Eastern Service Ribbon.

Kale M. Mills

ORAL W. MILLAR: Technical 5, U.S. Army. He was born January 4, 1922, in Lumberport. He was inducted on October 13, 1942, and honorably discharged on March 24, 1946. While serving he received the following awards: Asiatic-Pacific Theater Ribbon, Good Conduct Medal, and World War II Victory Medal. Headquarters Battery 198th F A Battalion.

Oral W. Millar

Arthur F. Miller

ARTHUR F. MILLER: Technical 4, U.S. Army, Company B, 116th Medical Battalion. He was born April 31, 1917, at Ivy. He was inducted on March 28, 1942, and honorably discharged on November 5, 1945. He served in Northern Solomons, Papuan and Southern Philippines. While serving he was awarded the following: Asiatic-Pacific Theater Ribbon with three Bronze Stars, Bronze Arrowhead Medal, Philippine Liberation Ribbon with one Bronze Star, and the Good Conduct Medal.

JAMES E. MILLER: Technical-4, U.S. Army, 652nd Tank Destroyer Battalion. He was born January 10, 1924, at Strader. He was inducted on March 8, 1943, and was honorably discharged on February 8, 1946. While serving he received the Good Conduct Medal and the American Theater service medal.

James E. Miller

Robert J. Miller

ROBERT JERRY MILLER: E-4, U.S. Army. He was born August 8, 1951, in Buckhannon. He was inducted January 28, 1971, and was discharged on January 27, 1977. While serving he received the National Defense Service Medal and Sharpshooter (M-16).

ROBERT LEWIS JUNIOR MORAN: E-5, U.S. Army. He was born April 4, 1945, in Century. He entered the service on March 29, 1966, and was discharged on October 27, 1970. He was awarded the following: National Defense Service Medal, Vietnam Service Medal, Vietnam Commendation Medal, Expert (M-14), and three Overseas Bars.

Robert L. J. Moran

DARIUS D. MORELAND: Corporal, Company K, 150th Infantry, U.S. Army. He was born March 6, 1912, in Buckhannon. He entered the service on September 20, 1943, and was honorably discharged on February 13, 1946. While serving he received the American Theater Service Medal, Asiatic-Pacific Service Medal, Good Conduct Medal, and World War II Victory Medal.

Darrell Moss

DARRELL MOSS: Private, U.S. Army. He was born in Queens. He was inducted September 15, 1942, and was honorably discharged June 15, 1943. He was discharged from the Enlisted Reserve Corps, U.S. Army on October 3, 1944. He served 336th Base Headquarters and Air Base Squadron, Buckley Field, Colorado.

GARY REX MOSS: Lance Corporal, U.S. Marine Corps. He died March 24, 1969, in Quang Nam Province (03), Republic of Vietnam, as a result of a gunshot wound to the body from hostile small arms fire while in a defensive position.

Gerald L. Moss

GERALD L. MOSS: Sergeant, U.S. Army. He joined the service in September 1949 and was discharged on October 6, 1952. He served in the Occupation of Japan and combat in Korea from July 4, 1950, to May 1, 1951, and won the Combat Infantry Badge and Korean Campaign Ribbon.

REX MOSS: Private First Class, Cannon Company, 121st Infantry, U.S. Army. He was born January 20, 1924, at Sago. He entered active duty on February 25, 1943, and was honorably discharged on November 2, 1945. He served in Normandy, Northern France, Rhineland and Central Europe. While serving he was awarded the Good Conduct Medal and the World War II Victory Medal.

Rex Moss

BERNARD L. MOYERS: Technical 5, Headquarters Battery 70 Development Artillery, U.S. Army. He was born April 18, 1919, in Pickens. He entered the service on August 12, 1942, and was honorably discharged on October 17, 1945. He served in Central Europe, Rhineland, Ardennes, Northern France, Normandy Campaign. He was awarded the following: Good Conduct Medal and European-African-Middle Eastern Service Medal with five Bronze Stars.

Bernard L. Moyers

RUSSELL LYELLE NEELEY: V-6, U.S. Navy, Ships Serviceman Barber Second Class. He was born December 31, 1911, at French Creek. He served NTS Norfolk, Virginia, RECSTA, Philadelphia, Pennsylvania, and USS *Tappahannock*. He enlisted on May 11, 1942, and was honorably discharged in October 1945.

Doris J. Nicely

DORIS J. NICELY (Rexroad): U.S. Air Force Airman First Class. She joined the service on January 17, 1951, and was honorably discharged on January 16, 1955, from Selfridge, Michigan. She did her basic training at Lackland A.F.B., San Antonio, Texas, schooling at Francis E. Warren in Cheyenne, Wyoming, duty at Kelly A.F.B. in San Antonio, Texas, as an Administration Specialist. She was stationed at Selfridge A.F.B. in budgeting and accounting. While serving she received the Commendation Ribbon.

DELF A. NORONA: Technical Fourth Class, U.S. Signal Corps. He enlisted at Fort Benjamin Harrison, Indiana, on September 17, 1942, and received thirteen weeks basic training and qualified on all hand weapons at Camp Crowder, Missouri. He was sent as cadre to the Western Signal Corps School, Davis, California, then transferred to the Corps of Engineer and departed San Francisco for the southwest and western Pacific on March 6, 1943. He served on Guadalcanal, BSI and other named and unnamed islands. He participated in the Luzon Campaign (Philippine Islands). He won the Bronze Star, Asiatic-Pacific Ribbon, American Theater Ribbon, Philippine Liberation Ribbon and the Victory Medal. He was discharged from Darnall General Hospital in Lexington, Kentucky, on November 23, 1945.

Edward L. Oldaker

EDWARD L. OLDAKER: Staff Sergeant, Headquarters and Headquarters Company, 93 ADG, U.S. Army Air Corps. He was born September 7, 1916, in Shinnston. He enlisted in the service on June 16, 1942, and was honorably discharged November 28, 1945. While serving he received the Good Conduct Medal, World War II Victory Medal, Asiatic-Pacific Theater Ribbon, and the American Theater Ribbon. He was awarded a Certificate of Commendable Service in appreciation of twenty-eight months of commendable service under conditions peculiar to the mainland and the Aleutian Islands of Alaska, requiring ingenuity, perseverance and devotion to duty.

GUY W. OSBORN: Master Sergeant, U.S. Air Force, Squadron B, 4112th AAF Base Unit. He was born March 19, 1917, in Gale. He enlisted on November 25, 1945, and was discharged the first time on May 24, 1947, then he re-enlisted, made Technical Sergeant on December 12, 1950. He retired from the service July 31, 1964. He was awarded the AFLSA with four Brass Oak Leaf Clusters and Good Conduct Medal.

Guy W. Osborn

RICHARD L. OURS: ASN RA 15069070, Headquarters Battery Second F.A. Battalion, Technical Sergeant. He served in Panama, Guatemala, England, France, Germany, and Holland. He received Battle Stars for Normandy, Southern France, Rhineland, and Central Europe, Battalion Communication Chief. His present address: 737 Embassy Pk., 2096 US-19-S, Clearwater, Florida 33546.

Cecil A. Page

CECIL ARDEN PAGE: Quartermaster Second Class (T), U.S. Navy. He was born March 17, 1922, in Selbyville. He entered the service on October 19, 1943. Served on *NTS GT Lakes,* Illinois, *Navtrascol,* Great Lakes, Illinois, *Phibtrabase,* Solomons, Maryland, *LCT* (5), Florida. While serving he was awarded the Pacific Theater Ribbon (one star), American Theater Ribbon, Victory Medal, and Philippine Liberation Ribbon. He was honorably discharged on January 4, 1946.

Miles W. Paugh

MILES W. PAUGH: Technical Sergeant, U.S. Air Force. He was born in Upshur County. He entered the army on July 19, 1948, and was honorably discharged on September 12, 1952, as a corporal. He then entered the Air Force on December 14, 1954, and retired on October 31, 1971. He served in Korea and Vietnam. He was awarded the Bronze Star Medal, Joint Service Commendation Medal, Presidential Unit Citation, Army Good Conduct Medal, Air Force Good Conduct Medal, Korean Service Medal with one Silver Star, National Defense Service Medal with one Star, Air Force Outstanding Award, Vietnam Service Medal, Air Force Longevity Service Award Ribbon with three Clusters, Small Arms Expert Marksmanship Ribbon, ROK Presidential Unit Citation, United Nations Service Medal, United Nations Medal, and Republic of Vietnam Campaign Medal.

MORGAN LEE PERRY: Sergeant First Class, U.S. Army. He was born August 7, 1928, in Buckhannon. He enlisted on December 14, 1950, and was honorably discharged on September 13, 1952. Battery C, 955th FA Battalion. While serving he was awarded the Korean Service Medal with three Bronze Camp Stars and the United Nations Service Medal.

BERNARD A. PHILLIPS: Staff Sergeant, Headquarters Company, First Infantry Regiment, Sixth Division, U.S. Army. He was born October 23, 1921, at French Creek. He entered the service on February 1, 1945, and was honorably discharged on August 9, 1946. While serving he received the Asiatic-Pacific Service Medal, Philippine Liberation Service Medal, Good Conduct Medal, World War II Victory Medal, and Occupation Medal, Japan.

Bernard A. Phillips

JOHN F. PHILLIPS: Private First Class, Battery "C," 771st Field Artillery Battalion, XII Corps, U.S. Army. He was born August 6, 1924, at French Creek. He was inducted on May 13, 1943, and honorably discharged on December 31, 1945. He served in Northern France, Rhineland, Ardennes and Central Europe. While serving he received the Good Conduct Medal, American Theater Service Medal, European-African-Middle Eastern Theater Service Medal with four Bronze Stars, and the Victory Medal.

RUSSELL RANDOLPH PHILLIPS: First Lieutenant, Corps of Engineers, U.S. Army, was honorably discharged on December 11, 1953.

SEWELL C. PHILLIPS: Corporal, Battery A, 283rd Field Artillery Battalion, U.S. Army. He was born June 12, 1914, at French Creek. He was inducted March 28, 1942, and was honorably discharged on March 12, 1945. While serving he received the European-African-Middle Eastern Theater Ribbon and the Good Conduct Medal.

Blaze R. Phipps

BLAZE RAY PHIPPS: Third Class, U.S. Navy. USS *Pugot Sound, Mediterranean,* Newport, Rhode Island, Norfolk, Virginia. He was born November 29, 1954, and deceased September 2, 1975.

EDGAR RAY PHIPPS: Sergeant, U.S. Marine Corps. He enlisted the first time in 1943-1946, then 1948-1952 and 1953-1955. He served in Guadalcanal, Guam, Okinawa and China. He was awarded the following: Presidential Unit Citation, Asiatic-Pacific Ribbon with two Stars, China Service Ribbon, and American Defense Award.

Edgar R. Phipps

PATRICK ALLEN PHIPPS: Third Class, U.S. Navy. He served from 1975 to 1979 on the aircraft carrier J.F. Kennedy on the Mediterranean Sea. He is now serving in the U.S. Army with E-4 rank in Fort Erwin, California. He enlisted September 1977.

Patrick A. Phipps

Selvia L. Phipps, Jr.

SELVIA LESTER PHIPPS, JR.: Corporal, #1257463, First School Company, Engineer Battalion, Marine Barracks, Camp Lejeune, North Carolina. He was awarded the National Defense Service Medal. He entered the service on December 5, 1951 and was discharged on December 2, 1953.

Gohen A. Pifer

GOHEN A. PIFER: Sergeant, U.S. Army. He was born January 21, 1921, in Buckhannon. He enlisted on August 1, 1940, and was discharged on October 11, 1945. He served in Luzon and New Guinea. While serving he received the Asiatic-Pacific Theater Ribbon with two Bronze Stars and the Philippines Liberation Ribbon with one Bronze Star.

GARELD POLING: Technical 5, Battery D, 951st AAA Auto. Weapons Battalion, U.S. Army. He was born September 21, 1921, at Ellamore. He went into active service on August 12, 1942. He served in the Northern Solomons and Luzon. While serving he received: Asiatic-Pacific Theater Ribbon with two Bronze Stars, Philippine Liberation Ribbon with one Bronze Service Star, Good Conduct Medal, and World War II Victory Medal. He was honorably discharged on December 11, 1945.

Gareld Poling

MERLIN D. POST: Staff Sergeant, Armour Service Infantry. He was born December 23, 1918. He served in the Aleutian Islands and Rhineland. He also served in Alaska and France. He was a sharpshooter with M-1 rifle and was awarded the Combat Infantryman's Badge. While serving he was awarded the Good Conduct Medal, American Defense Service Medal with one Bronze Star, Asiatic-Pacific Service Medal, and European-African-Middle Eastern Service Medal. He died March 10, 1986.

Merlin D. Post

HAROLD CLAIR PUMPHREY: Sergeant First Class, U.S. Army. He was born February 25, 1929, in Buckhannon. He entered the service in November 1946. He served four tours of duty in Germany and two tours of duty in Korea. While serving he received the Army Commendation Medal. He died on April 13, 1969.

Clifton L. Queen

CLIFTON LeROY QUEEN: Seaman First Class V 6, U.S. Navy. He was born on May 18, 1927, in Buckhannon. He enlisted in the service on May 3, 1945, and was honorably discharged on August 10, 1946. He served on these vessels: NTC, Great Lakes, Illinois USS *Prevail*, USS *YMS473* and USS *Buckeye*. He was awarded the Pacific Theater Ribbon, American Theater Ribbon, and the Victory Medal.

French W. Queen, Jr.

FRENCH W. QUEEN, JR.: Technical 5, U.S. Army, 967th ORD HAM Company. He was born December 11, 1925, in Buckhannon. He was inducted on July 23, 1944, and was honorably discharged on October 31, 1946. While serving he received the Asiatic-Pacific Service Medal, Good Conduct Medal, World War II Victory Medal, and Occupation Ribbon (Japan).

CHARLES WILLIAM RATCLIFF: Corporal, U.S. Marine Corps. He was born on October 25, 1930, in Lewis County. He was inducted on February 20, 1952, and honorably discharged on February 19, 1954. While serving he was awarded the National Defense Ribbon.

CLARENCE EDWARD RATCLIFF: Private First Class, U.S. Marine Corps. He was born November 19, 1923, in Weston. He enlisted in the service March 8, 1943, and was honorably discharged December 18, 1945. He served in the Pacific area. He participated in action against the enemy at Guam, Mariana Islands, Iwo Jima and Volcano Islands. He was issued Honorable Service Lapel Button and Good Conduct Medal.

JASON RATCLIFF: Private First Class, 305th F Signal Battalion. He was born in Ivanhoe. He enlisted March 31, 1918. He served in the Somme App. Artois Sector from July 23 to August 18, 1918, St. Mihiel Offensive September 12-14, 1918, Meuse-Argonne Offensive September 26 to October 12 and November 1-7, 1918. He was honorably discharged June 7, 1919.

PAUL D. RATCLIFF: Specialist 5, U.S. Army. He was honorably discharged from duty on August 31, 1967.

ROBERT L. RATCLIFF: Sergeant, U.S. Army. He was born September 17, 1927, in Weston. He enlisted October 25, 1945, and was discharged March 30, 1948. While serving his country he received the World War II Victory Medal. He was honorably discharged.

CORBIN EUGENE REED: Corporal, U.S. Marine Corps. He was born September 7, 1924, in Buckhannon. He enlisted on May 10, 1943, and was honorably discharged on February 15, 1946. He participated in action against the enemy at Guam, Mariana Islands from July 21 to August 15, 1944, Okinawa, Ryukyu Islands from April 1 to June 21, 1945, and in the occupation of China from October 3, 1945 to January 14, 1946. He was awarded the Good Conduct Medal.

DEAN M. REED: Staff Sergeant, 211th Hospital Ship Complement, U.S. Army. He was born July 26, 1917, at Tallmansville. He entered the service on March 15, 1943, and was honorably discharged on October 6, 1945. He served in Naples-Foggia, Southern France, Luzon, Philippines, Southern Philippines and New Guinea. He received the following awards: Good Conduct Medal, Philippine Liberation Ribbon with one Bronze Star, American Campaign Medal, Asiatic-Pacific Campaign Medal, European-African-Middle Eastern Campaign Medal.

Dean M. Reed

Donald E. Reed

DONALD E. REED: Staff Sergeant, U.S. Air Force. He was born June 28, 1922. He entered the service on October 16, 1942. He served in the South Pacific. He was declared missing in action over Yap Island on July 5, 1944. He was awarded the Air Medal with eight Oak Leaf Clusters and the Purple Heart.

FORMAN R. REED: Corporal, 2523rd AAF Base Unit, U.S. Army. He was born July 14, 1923, in Buckhannon. He was inducted on January 4, 1943. He was awarded numerous medals, etc., while serving: American Theater Ribbon, Good Conduct Medals, World War II Victory Medal, Korean Service Medal with two Brass Stars, United Nations Service Medal, National Defense Service Medal, ROK Presidential Unit Citation, National Defense Service Medal with one Bronze Service Star, Republic of Vietnam Campaign Medal, Good Conduct Medal with one Brass Oak Leaf Cluster, AF Outstanding Unit Award and AF Longevity Service Award with four Bronze Oak Leaf Clusters. He joined the Air Force in December of 1950 and made a career of it. He was an honor student from the Spartan School of Aeronautics, he completed the course for Airplane Mechanics on June 29, 1943, the Aircraft Maintenance Technical Course on November 28,

Forman R. Reed

1958, the Maintenance Documentation Course on January 9, 1959, the Automotive Repairman Course on August 8, 1960, three more courses on Aircraft Maintenance (March 2, 1965, March 4, 1966 and May 11, 1967). He now lives in Buckhannon.

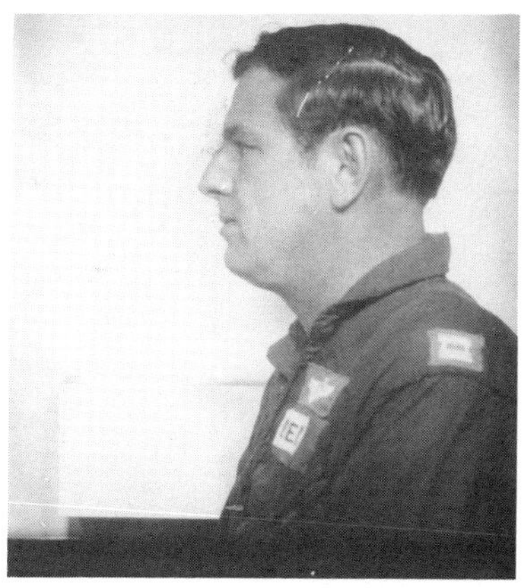
Gerald M. Reed

GERALD MARK REED: Staff Sergeant, U.S. Air Force. He was born November 6, 1935. While serving he was awarded: Distinguished Flying Cross, Air Medal with twelve Oak Leaf Clusters, AF Good Conduct Medal, Small Arms Expert Marksmanship Ribbon, Marine Corps Good Conduct Medal, Combat Readiness Medal, AF Longevity Service Award with four Oak Leaf Clusters, National Defense Service Medal, Vietnam Service Medal with seven devices, AF Outstanding Unit Award, Republic of Vietnam Gallantry Cross with one Device, and Republic of Vietnam Campaign Medal.

Paul Freeman Reed

PAUL FREEMAN REED: WT Third Class, U.S. Navy. He was born October 28, 1925, in Red Rock. He entered active duty on December 20, 1943. He was discharged on May 21, 1946. He served in the Mariana Islands (Guam, Tinian and Saipan), Philippine Sea Battle, Iwo Jima and Okinawa. While serving he was awarded the following: Pacific Theater Ribbon with three Stars, American Theater Ribbon, Victory Medal, Philippine Liberation Ribbon, and Presidential Unit Citation with One Star. He served on the *NTS Great Lakes,* Illinois, USS *Wadsworth.*

REX B. REED: Private, U.S. Army. He was born in Tallmansville. He was inducted on October 13, 1942. He was discharged on March 23, 1943.

Rex B. Reed

CLARENCE H. REEDER: Private, U.S. Army. He was born in Buckhannon. He was inducted April 26, 1918. He served in the Meuse-Argonne Offensive from September 26, 1918, to October 1, 1918. He was honorably discharged on April 7, 1919.

Clarence H. Reeder

Charles E. Reger, Jr.

CHARLES E. REGER, JR.: Private First Class, 48th Tank Battalion, U.S. Army. He was born September 27, 1919, at Adrian. He was inducted on March 28, 1942, and was honorably discharged on September 28, 1945. He served in Naples-Foggia, Rome-Arno, Southern France, Rhineland, and Central Europe. He was awarded the following: Good Conduct Medal and the European-African-Middle Eastern Service Ribbon with One Bronze Arrowhead.

Esker W. Rice

ESKER W. RICE: Technical Fourth Grade, U.S. Army, 113th AAA Group Headquarters. He was born October 1, 1917, in Buckhannon. He entered active duty on November 30, 1942, and was honorably discharged on October 26, 1945. He served in Normandy, Northern France, Ardennes, Rhineland, and Central Europe. He was awarded the Good Conduct Medal and the European-African-Middle Eastern Ribbon.

WILLARD H. RICE: Private, Cavalry, U.S. Army. He was born July 23, 1908, at Canaan. He entered active duty on February 23, 1945. Reason for separation: Certificate of disability for discharge.

Willard H. Rice

MORRIS EDWARD RINGER: Aviation-Metalsmith First Class, U.S. Navy. He was born September 13, 1916, at Abbott. He enlisted in the service December 28, 1939. Ratings held: AS, S2/c, S1/c, AM2/c, AM1/c and AM3/c. He served on the following vessels: *NTS, NOB,* Norfolk, Virginia, *USNAS,* Pensacola, Florida, Patrol Sqd. #26, Patrol Sqd. #102, 16th N.D., and Fourth Marines. He was awarded the following medals, ribbons, etc.: ALVAV 76-46, Pacific Theater Ribbon with One Star, Good Conduct Ribbon, Philippine Liberation Ribbon with One Star, Philippine Defense Ribbon, Army Dist. Unit Badge with Oak Leaf, American Theater Ribbon, Victory Medal, and Presidential Unit Citation with One Star.

Morris E. Ringer

Dairel W. Rowan

DAIREL W. ROWAN: Pharmacist's Mate Third Class, U.S. Navy. He joined the service on August 2, 1943, and was discharged on May 12, 1946. He went to boot camp, Great Lakes, *NLS,* Corps School, Great Lakes, *NLS,* Hospital Training, Mare Island, California. He also had additional training in California. He served in Okinawa and the Philippines. He was awarded the Pacific Theater Ribbon with One Star, American Theater Ribbon and the Victory Medal.

Delmar F. Rowan

DELMAR FRIEL ROWAN: Aviation Machinist's Mate Third Class, U.S. Navy. He was born August 9, 1922, at Hesper. He served *NRS,* Clarksburg, West Virginia, *NTS,* Great Lakes, Illinois, RS, SO Annex Nob, Norfolk, Virginia, Casu No. 32 (Air Transport Squadron Four), RS, San Diego, California and NRS, Pittsburgh, Pennsylvania. He received the Pacific Theater Ribbon, American Theater Ribbon, and the Victory Medal. He was honorably discharged on January 2, 1946.

JEARL ROBERT ROWAN: E-4, U.S. Army. He was born September 7, 1948, in Buckhannon. He entered the service on October 29, 1965, and was discharged on October 28, 1971. While serving he was awarded the National Defense Service Medal, Good Conduct Medal, and the PRCHT Badge.

ROBERT H. RUTHERFORD: Sergeant, 378th Harbor Craft Company. He was born on July 21, 1914, at Lewisburg. He enlisted in the U.S. Army December 11, 1940, and was honorably discharged August 6, 1945. While serving in the army he served in the Southern Philippines. He was awarded the American Defense Service Medal with One Bronze Star, American Service Medal,

Robert H. Rutherford

Asiatic-Pacific Service Ribbon and Philippines Liberation Ribbon. He then joined the U.S. Air Force on January 11, 1946, and was honorably discharged as sergeant from that branch on January 18, 1949. He was awarded the World War II Victory Medal.

ORVAL MICHAEL RYAN: E-5, U.S. Army. Headquarters and Company A, 707th Maintenance Battalion, Seventh Infantry Division, Eighth Army. He was born November 18, 1948, in Buckhannon. He was discharged April 21, 1975.

ROBERT M. SANDY: Private First Class, U.S. Army, Infantry. He served in active duty from April 9, 1953, to April 8, 1955.

Robert M. Sandy

Charles J. See

CHARLES JUNIOR SEE: Seaman First Class, U.S. Navy. He was born October 14, 1924, at Adrian. He entered active service August 2, 1943, and was honorably discharged May 7, 1946. He served on the *USNTS* Great Lakes, Illinois, *USNAS*, Minneapolis, Minnesota, *USNB*, TESI. He was awarded the Pacific Theater Ribbon, American Theater Ribbon, and Victory Medal.

Charley See

CHARLEY SEE: Private, Company M-168, Infantry, U.S. Army. He was inducted on June 26, 1918, and was honorably discharged on May 13, 1919. He served in the Army of Occupation from December 12, 1918, to April 1, 1919.

RUSKIN R. SHAHAN: Corporal, U.S. Air Force, 78th AAF Base Unit. He was born October 24, 1917, at Czar. He entered active duty on September 8, 1943, and was honorably discharged March 13, 1946. While serving he was awarded the following: Good Conduct Medal, American Theater Ribbon, and World War II Victory Ribbon.

Ruskin R. Shahan

WILLIAM LAWRENCE SHEPPARD: Boatswain's Mate Second Class, U.S. Navy. He was born September 23, 1923, in Palestine. He was inducted on May 10, 1943, and honorably discharged on February 13, 1946. He served in New Guinea and the Schouten Islands (made up of Biak, Owi and Woendi). While serving he was awarded the following: Pacific Theater Ribbon, American Theater Ribbon, and Victory Medal.

William L. Sheppard

David H. Shobe

DAVID HUGH SHOBE: Private First Class, E-3, U.S. Army, Headquarters Battery B, 8th Battalion, 3d ADA. He was born April 13, 1950, in Weston. He was inducted May 26, 1970, and was discharged May 25, 1976. While serving he received the National Defense Service Medal and the Presidential Unit Citation. He completed eight weeks of advanced individual training in MOS 16B10 Air Defense Launcher Crewman (Nick Hercules in Fort Bliss, Texas). He received a Certificate of Appreciation for active service on January 13, 1972. He served in the Thirtieth Artillery Brigade as a launcher crewman at Fort Buckner, Okinawa.

Marion B. Shobe

MARION B. SHOBE: Sergeant, U.S. Army, Company B, Fifty-fifth Armored Infantry Battalion. He was born May 19, 1924, in Upshur County. He was inducted June 21, 1943, and was honorably discharged January 20, 1946. He served in Ardennes and Rhineland. He received a Good Conduct Medal, Purple Heart Medal, American Theater Ribbon, European-African-Middle Eastern Theater Ribbon, and World War II Victory Ribbon.

ROBERT BURTON SHOBE: RCT E-1 (P), U.S. Army Recruit AUS. He was born January 24, 1937, at Streight Forks. He was inducted November 28, 1960, and honorably discharged August 23, 1966.

WILLIAM FREDERICK SHOBE: E-4, U.S. Army. He was born April 14, 1947, in Buckhannon. He was inducted April 16, 1968, and discharged April 15, 1974. While serving he received the National Defense Medal, Vietnam Service Medal, Vietnam Commendation Medal, Army Commendation Medal, BS Medal, Good Conduct Medal, and two Overseas Bars. He completed a field radio mechanic course on August 23 at the Armored School, Fort Knox, Kentucky. On August 6, 1970, he was awarded the Certificate of Appreciation for active service and faithful duty.

William F. Shobe

WILLIAM THOMAS SHOBE: Corporal (T), U.S. Army. He was born April 12, 1933, in Upshur County. He was inducted May 27, 1953, and was honorably discharged on May 31, 1961. While serving he received the National Defense Medal, Korean Service Medal, United Nation Service Medal, and Good Conduct Medal.

William T. Shobe

Enoch R. Shreve

ENOCH RALPH SHREVE: Private First Class, U.S. Army. He was born October 21, 1922, in Buckhannon. He entered active service January 1, 1943, and was discharged February 3, 1946. He was a Military Police in the Army. He patrolled cities, apprehended black market operators, maintained order, checked passes, guarded military installations and prisoners of war. He was assigned to the 258th Military Police Company in the European Theater. He served in England, Scotland, France, and Czechoslovakia. While serving he received the Good Conduct Medal, American Theater Ribbon, European-African-Middle Eastern Theater Ribbon, and World War II Victory Ribbon. His present address is: 41 Vicksburg Rd., Buckhannon, West Virginia 26201.

JOHN A. SHREVE: Private First Class, U.S. Army. He joined on May 12, 1942, and was discharged on October 18, 1945. He served for ten and one-half months in Germany ETO in the Ninety-fifth Infantry Division. He was wounded on December 2, 1944. He served in England, France, and Germany. He was awarded three Battle Stars, Bronze Star and a Good Conduct Medal.

James P. Simon

JAMES P. SIMON: Served in the U.S. Navy from September 1946 to September 1956. He took basic training at Great Lakes, Illinois. He was stationed at Naval Communications Station, Washington, D.C., Arlington Hall Station, Arlington, Virginia, Naval Radio Station, Skaggs Island, California, Naval Radio Station, Yokosuka, Japan, Naval Radio Station, Kami Seya, Japan, Eleventh Naval Distribution Headquarters, San Diego, California, and U.S. Naval Training Center, San Diego, California. While serving he earned the Good Conduct Medal, World War II Victory Medal, American Area Medal, National Defense Service Medal, Korean Service Medal, United Nations Service Medal, and two Unit Citations.

LONNIE SIMONS: Private First Class, Infantry, Company H, 175th Infantry Regiment APO 29. He was born November 8, 1924, in Buckhannon. He entered service duty July 9, 1943, and was discharged December 9, 1945. He served in Normandy, Northern France, Ardennes, Rhineland and Central Europe. He was awarded the European-African-Middle Eastern Ribbon and the Good Conduct Medal.

ROBERT S. SIMONS: Private First Class, Detachment Medical Department, Twenty-ninth Evacuation Hospital, U.S. Army. He was honorably discharged March 14, 1944.

Robert S. Simons

Adon R. Simmons

ADON R. SIMMONS: Private First Class, Fortieth FA Group, U.S. Army. He was born April 18, 1926, at Alton. He entered active service September 13, 1944, and was honorably discharged October 31, 1945. He served in Central Europe. He was awarded the following: European-African-Middle Eastern Ribbon, Bronze Service Star, and Central Europe.

Dorsey J. Simmons

DORSEY J. SIMMONS: Private First Class, Company B, 133rd Engineer Combat Battalion, U.S. Army. He was born October 12, 1923, at Alton. He entered active service on July 5, 1943, and was honorably discharged December 16, 1945. He served in Normandy, Northern France, Ardennes, Rhineland, and Central Europe. He earned the Good Conduct Medal, Purple Heart Medal, European-African-Middle Eastern Theater Ribbon, and World War II Victory Ribbon.

FREEMAN D. SIMMONS: Cook, Company B, 103rd Battalion, U.S. Army. He was born in Hemlock. He served in Company C, First Regiment Infantry, West Virginia National Guard from May 28, 1917, to August 5, 1917. He served in France. He left the United States October 2, 1918, and returned April 17, 1919.

Freeman D. Simmons

JAMES GALE SKINNER: E-8, Sergeant, U.S. Air Force, 335th Armament and Electrical Maintenance Squadron (TAC). He was born December 12, 1923, in Hettie. He entered the service January 23, 1957. He had two prior enlistments. He was honorably discharged. From February 1943 to November 1945 he served with the Forty-fourth Infantry Division,

U.S. Army. He was in combat in Europe for ten months and twenty days. He received three Battle Stars and Bronze Star. He also received the Good Conduct Medal, Bronze C1 with 2 lapels, AFLS Award with three Oak Leaf Clusters, Good Conduct Medal with three Bronze Lps, AFLSA with four Bronze Oak Leaf Clusters, National Defense Medal United Nations Service Medal, Korean Service Medal and Commendation Ribbon.

James G. Skinner

Joey D. Slaughter

JOEY DALE SLAUGHTER: Aviation Electrician's Mate, Third Class, U.S. Navy. He was born February 19, 1924, in Buckhannon. He enlisted November 19, 1942, and was honorably discharged January 25, 1946. He served on the *USNTS*, Great Lakes, Illinois, *HedRon FAW 11, HedRon FAW 12,* Patsu Supporting VB 130, CASU (F) 62, NAS, Alameda, California, and Boca Chica, Florida. He was awarded the Philippine Liberation with one Star, Asiatic-Pacific, American Theater, and Victory Medal.

Evert S. Smith

EVERT S. SMITH: U.S. Army, World War II. He was born June 9, 1917, in Buckhannon. He went into active duty September 29, 1943, and was discharged February 19, 1946.

HAYWARD C. SMITH: U.S. Army, World War II. He entered the service in 1942 and was discharged in 1946. He served in England. He was a tailgunner on a B-52.

Hayward C. Smith

JAMES McWHORTER SMITH: Private First Class, U.S. Army. He was born February 6, 1929, in Buckhannon. He entered active service March 20, 1951, and was honorably discharged March 7, 1953, and transferred to ERC. His most significant duty assignment was Moji Port 8156th AU. While serving he was awarded the Korean Service Medal with one Bronze Service Star and the United Nations Service Medal.

James M. Smith

JAMES O. SMITH: Private First Class, Medical Detachment, Eighth Infantry, U.S. Army. He was born April 2, 1913, in Queens. He was inducted May 13, 1942, and was honorably discharged September 19, 1945. He served in Northern France, Ardennes, Central Europe, Normandy and Rhineland. While serving he earned the Bronze Star Medal, the Purple Heart, Presidential Unit Citation, Good Conduct Medal, Medical Badge, and European-African-Middle Eastern Theater Ribbon with five Bronze Battle Stars.

LOYAL E. SMITH: Private First Class, U.S. Army. He was born in Abbott. He enlisted May 15, 1918. He served in England and France. He returned to the U.S. July 10, 1919. He was honorably discharged on July 18, 1919.

William E. Smith

WILLIAM E. SMITH: Private First Class, U.S. Air Force, 323rd AAF Base Unit. He was born March 7, 1924, in Buckhannon. He went into active service August 16, 1943. He served in Normandy, Northern France, Ardennes, Rhineland, Central Europe, Air Offensive Europe, Air Combat France. He was awarded the following: European-African-Middle Eastern Theater Ribbon with one Silver Star and two Bronze Stars, Good Conduct Medal, Distinguished Unit Badge. He was honorably discharged October 27, 1945.

JUDSON DUAINE SPORE: E-4, U.S. Army. He was born June 8, 1945, in Gilmer County. He was inducted October 14, 1965, and was discharged October 13, 1971. While serving he was awarded the Good Conduct Medal and National Defense Service Medal.

Judson D. Spore

CLIFFORD K. STOCKERT: Sergeant, U.S. Army. He was born in Buckhannon, on June 30, 1898. He enlisted on April 28, 1917. He died at Camp Hancock, Augusta, Georgia, on October 11, 1918. He was Machine Gun Instructor of Training Co. No. 16 Machine Gun Training Center, Main Training Depot, 4th Bn., Group 2, Camp Hancock. At his death he was a sergeant, but was to have been commissioned to lieutenant on the following day.

Clifford K. Stockert

Thomas L. Stockert, Jr.

THOMAS L. STOCKERT, JR.: Staff Sergeant, Security Intelligence Corps Headquarters, Fifth Service Company. He was born July 11, 1913, in Buckhannon. He was inducted on July 29, 1942, and was honorably discharged on February 7, 1946. While serving he received the American Theater Ribbon, Good Conduct Medal, Victory Medal World War II and the Meritorious Unit Award.

Arnold G. Swick

ARNOLD G. SWICK: Staff Sergeant, 182nd Medical Detachment, 182nd Ordnance Battalion. He was born November 4, 1923, at Ellamore. He went into active service August 16, 1943, and was honorably discharged January 9, 1946. He served in Normandy, Northern France, Rhineland, and Central Europe. He was awarded the Good Conduct Medal, European-African-Middle Eastern Theater Ribbon, and World War II Victory Ribbon.

William O. Swick

WILLIAM O. SWICK: Corporal, Medical Detachment, U.S. Army. He was born in West Virginia. He enlisted March 3, 1918. He served in A.E.F. from May 19, 1918, to August 20, 1919. He was honorably discharged August 26, 1919. "William Swick, of near Gale, who went to France some time ago attached to a hospital corps, was a member of hospital crew that returned to America two weeks ago with a number of incapacitated Americans among whom were sixteen insane men, who has lost their reason by gas poisoning. Mr. Swick secured a leave of absence on arriving in New York and came on to visit his home folks. He tells some harrowing and interesting incidents coming under his personal observation while in France. He said during the voyage to America that his hospital ship was attacked by five submarines and he was an eye witness to the sinking of three of the number and was not certain whether they succeeded in making good their escape. In any event they were not bothered by any more subs during the trip."

Following is a poem dedicated to Our Boys that Served in the Armed Forces. It was written by Leta Lamb of Ellamore.

We've gathered tonight to honor our boys,
Who are scattered afar as the Army employees.
Some are in the East and some in the West,
They follow the flag where the commander sees best.
We're lonely without them and, Please God, speed the day,
That brings our boys home, each one that's away.
On that mission of honor and justice and right,
God grant us more courage and our armies more might,
That will enable us soon to be victorious, and then,
The boys who have left us will come back as men.
Don't let them be hardened and bitter because
We perhaps have not lived as we should.
So, just pause for a moment and ask yourself this:
Have I took time each day, just a moment to pray,
That God will take care of my son who's away?
Have I gathered up paper? Have I saved the waste fat?
Have I bought Victory Bonds? Have I done this or that?
If we are found wanting on the Home Front, can they
Come back to us with: What a price we did pay
For our way of life, for the privilege to say,
What we wish to, To preach and to pray where we will.
Our life's blood run red. Did you do your share
While we were all fighting and dying out there?
If our answer is "no," let us pause and think deep,
Was it really worthwhile these privileges to seep,
That they fought and died? Are we standing by,
While their souls are being tried?
Our Boys:
There are Glenville and Warren, John, Howard and Paul,
Vern Earl, Mason and Orbed, we pray for them all.

Then, there's Junior and Denver, Kermit, Ancil and Sam,
Buddie Lewis, Don and Ralph Shipman, and the whole Riley clan.
Bud, James, Joe, Bill and Harry,
When a war's being fought, they could not at home tarry.
There is Glenville McDonald, and Poland's one son,
Arnold Swick, Rex Lamb, Arnold Lamb—Oh! the list is just begun.
There's Ben Booth and Marvin, Luther Roy and Jim,
Earl and Rex Moss, we must not forget them.
Then, the McCauleys: Russell, Hartsel and Woodrow,
Bob Darnall, Johnnie Shehan—Oh, they all had to go.
John Moore and Ed Hamlin and Joan Moore Green,
The one girl on the list, so she shall be queen.
Clyde McCord, John Connors, Warren Gower, Verlin and Marvel
Cutright, Burl and Carl Newlon, let them stand for the right.
Then there's the Koons: Mack, Virgil and Rex, Bud Davis,
John Wentz, Wratchfords, Charlie and Pat, Loyal Phillips,
Carleton Liller—We just pick them in spots, Oh yes, don't
Forget there is "Hop" and Raymond Watts, And, Ray Osburn too,
And Clint Shreve and John. I thought I was through, but now
And anon, there are other names flashing alight on my mind.
The Harris boys—Carl "Super" and Joe,
The Heater boys and Junior Furman, They all had to go.
Then there was Charles Dolan and Rudy Zirbs too,
Who went to the Navy to see what they could do.
Bayard Jack, Theodore Jack, the Nesbitts, Bob and Russell are seen
There's the Smiths, Jack and Phil, and there is Keith Queen.
Then the other Smith boys, James and Brent,
Howard Bodkin, Jimmy Dice, Junior Caynor, to the Army were sent.
Jamie Cregler, Sylvester Robinson and Tony Cappadony,
Harry Fraley and Vernon Robinson, the last on the list,
From each of their homes, how these boys are missed.

As we look on the flag with its stars so blue,
We think of our boys with hearts so true.
The summer is waning, the days growing cold,
God, keep the stars blue—Don't let one turn to gold.

Morris V. Tallman

MORRIS V. TALLMAN: Private First Class, Seventh AAA AW Battalion, U.S. Army. He was born October 3, 1920, in Buckhannon. He entered active service August 12, 1942, and was honorably discharged January 5, 1946. He served in Eastern Mandates, Western Pacific, Southern Philippines (Liberation) and Ryukyus. While serving he earned the following awards: Asiatic-Pacific Theater Ribbon with three Bronze Stars, Philippine Liberation Ribbon with one Bronze Star, and American Theater Ribbon.

Victor R. Tallman

VICTOR ROLLAND TALLMAN: Signalman Third Class (T), U.S. Navy. He was born April 7, 1925, at Ten Mile. He entered active service July 12, 1943. He served on *USNTS*, Great Lakes, Illinois, Communication Scol. Phil-Train-Pac, ABRD, IROGUOIS PT, COMSERVPAC, ADVBASE-COMCOMMTRACENTER Comm Unit 17, CUB 12 COMM UNIT 431 Comp. C-8 (52), NavSta, Navy 3149, USNB, Navy 3002. While serving he received the Pacific Theater Ribbon with one Star, American Theater Ribbon, Victory Medal, the Philippine Liberation Ribbon with one Star, Asiatic-Pacific Theater Medal, American Theater Medal, and World War II Victory Medal.

Charles N. Taylor

CHARLES N. TAYLOR: Sergeant, Company C, 20th Infantry Regiment, U.S. Army. He was born November 22, 1924, in Parkersburg. He was inducted January 31, 1945, and honorably discharged on December 12, 1946. While serving he received the following: Asiatic-Pacific Service Medal, World War II Victory Medal, Philippine Liberation Service Medal, Good Conduct Medal, and Occupation Medal Japan.

DONALD LEE TEETS: E-2, U.S. Marine Corps. He was born September 16, 1944, in Ravenna, Ohio. Company B, ScolsDemTrsm MCS, Quantico, Virginia. He entered the service September 29, 1961, and was discharged March 19, 1968. While serving he was awarded the National Defense Service Medal, Pistol Sharpshooter Badge, Caliber .45 and Rifle Sharpshooter, M-14.

Donald L. Teets

HARRY JEFFERSON TEETS: Staff Sergeant, U.S. Army, 24th Infantry Division. He was born December 19, 1918, at Ivanhoe. He joined the service on February 2, 1945, and was discharged October 23, 1946.

Harry J. Teets

Norman M. Teets

NORMAN MURRAY TEETS: U.S. Army Reserve, Company B, 197th Tk. Battalion. He joined the Reserves March 20, 1957. He was born March 2, 1940, in Buckhannon. He entered the U.S. Air Force in 1958. He was honorably discharged November 5, 1970. While serving he completed a Refrigeration Specialist Course (refrigeration and air conditioning). He was awarded the Outstanding Unit Award, 4123rd Strategic Wing (heavy). He was also awarded the Good Conduct Medal and Longevity Medal. He served in the Berlin Crisis, Cuban Crisis, Asia and Vietnam.

Dennis M. Tenney

DENNIS MAYNARD TENNEY: U.S. Army. He entered the service in 1943 and was discharged in 1946. He served in the Philippines as a Medical Technician.

EDGAR TENNEY: U.S. Army. He entered the service in 1943 and was discharged in 1946. He served in England. He served as guard for General Dwight D. Eisenhower.

Edgar Tenney

ISRAEL R. TENNEY: Staff Sergeant, Company B, 393rd Infantry, Ninety-ninth Division, U.S. Army. He was born January 27, 1915, at Sand Run. He entered active service December 9, 1942, and was honorably discharged February 17, 1946. He served in Ardennes and Rhineland. While serving he was awarded the Good Conduct Medal, American Theater Ribbon, European-African-Middle Eastern Theater Ribbon, and World War II Victory Ribbon.

Israel R. Tenney

James F. Tenney

JAMES F. TENNEY: Private, Headquarters Company, 351st Infantry, U.S. Army. He was born March 2, 1913, in Pickens. He was inducted June 5, 1942, and honorably discharged September 11, 1945. He served in Naples-Foggia, Northern Apennines and Po Valley. While serving he received the Good Conduct Medal and the European-African-Middle Eastern Service Ribbon.

Junior L. Tenney

JUNIOR LLOYD TENNEY: U.S. Navy. He entered the service in 1943 and was discharged in 1946. He served on the *Saratoga*. He was on board when the ship was bombed.

SILAS E. TENNEY: Technical 4, U.S. Army. He was born December 24, 1912, at Sand Run. He entered active service March 28, 1942, and was honorably discharged August 27, 1945. 2755th Engineer Combat Battalion. He served in Scotland, England, North Africa, Italy, France, and Germany. He served with the Fifth and Seventh Army.

Silas E. Tenney

VIRGIL TENNEY: Technical 4, U.S. Army, Company A, 321st Medical Battalion, 96th Infantry Division. He was born February 17, 1919, at Tallmansville. He entered active service May 13, 1942, and was honorably discharged January 15, 1946. He served in the Southern Philippines (Liberation) and Ryukyus. While serving he received the following: Asiatic-Pacific Theater Ribbon with two Bronze Service Stars, Philippine Liberation Ribbon with two Bronze Service Stars, Bronze Star Medal, and Meritorious Unit Award with Gold Star.

Virgil Tenney

Loy R. Thomas

LOY R. THOMAS: Private First Class, U.S. Army. He was born February 12, 1910, at French Creek. He was inducted on January 16, 1941. He served with Company H, Fifty-first Infantry. He was honorably discharged on December 31, 1942. He passed away August 18, 1987, Veterans Administration Hospital, Clarksburg.

Ralph E. Travis

RALPH E. TRAVIS: Corporal, U.S. Army, Headquarters Company, Third Battalion, First Infantry. He took basic training at Fort Leonard Wood, Mississippi, in August 1942. He was then sent to the Yuma Desert for desert training in North Africa. When the tide of the war there changed, he was sent to Hawaii for jungle training. He was sent first to New Guinea and was involved in those campaigns, then on to the Philippines. He was killed in Rizal, the mountains above Manila. He received the Purple Heart.

DAVID LINN WAGGY: First Lieutenant. He enlisted in 1967 at Beckley, West Virginia, and was discharged on March 8, 1970. He served in the Seventh Division in Korea from 1969 to 1970. Nearest relative is Bob Waggy of Buckhannon.

David L. Waggy

ROBERT H. WAGGY: Sergeant, "Air Apaches," Fifth Air Force, Turret Gunner on B-25. He entered the service in March 1943 and completed his training in radio repair at Camp Crowder, Missouri, and the Air Force Armament School at Lowry Field, Denver, Colorado. He received his gunner's wings at Fort Myers, Florida. He was assigned to overseas duty in November 1944 in Luzon, Leyte Island, Philippines. He was killed in the South Pacific on March 15, 1945.

Robert H. Waggy

Wilbert T. Wagner

WILBERT T. WAGNER: Private First Class, U.S. Army, Company C, 115th Infantry. He was born August 19, 1924, at Hall. He entered active service October 18, 1943, and was honorably discharged January 21, 1946. He served in Normandy, Northern France, Rhineland, and Central Europe. He received the Good Conduct Medal, Purple Heart Medal, European-African-Middle Eastern Theater Ribbon with Bronze Arrowhead, Distinguished Unit Badge and World War II Victory Ribbon. He was a member of Twenty-ninth Infantry Division on D Day, June 6, 1944, and served with it continuously until the capture of St. Lo on July 18, 1944.

RICHARD KARROL WAMSLEY: E-3, U.S. Navy. He was born October 4, 1943, at Ellamore. He entered the service March 14, 1956, and was discharged March 13, 1962. He received the Good Conduct Medal.

I. J. Warner

I. J. WARNER: U.S. Navy. He enlisted in 1943. He served on LST 735, Pacific Rhode Island, HDV for three years. He served in Henrico and Subic Bay. He was discharged at Bethesda Naval Hospital, Maryland, in 1966.

WILLIAM H. WATTS: Corporal, U.S. Army, Company A, 313th Engineering (C) Battalion. He was born February 27, 1917, at Ellamore. He was inducted June 17, 1942, and was honorably discharged October 7, 1945. He served in Tunisia, Naples-Foggia, Rome-Arno, North Apennines and Po Valley. He received the Good Conduct Medal and the European-African-Middle Eastern Service Ribbon.

CHARLES STANLEY WAUGAMAN: Seaman First Class, U.S. Navy. He was born July 2, 1921, in Buckhannon. He entered active service on October 4, 1943. He served NTS Great Lakes, Illinois, CASU #38, USS *Princeton* and USS *Columbus* (CA-74). He was honorably discharged on January 10, 1946. While serving he received the Pacific Theater Ribbon, American Theater Ribbon, the Victory Medal, the Philippine Liberation with two Stars, Pacific Ribbon, five Bronze Stars. Survivor of Sinking of *Princeton*.

Charles S. Waugaman

JOHN WILLARD WAYTS: Airman Third Class, U.S. Air Force, Clerk Helper. He was born October 26, 1934, at Alton. He enlisted September 18, 1952, and was honorably discharged November 18, 1953. He was assigned to 2225th Pers. Proc. Gp., Camp Kilmer, New Jersey.

John W. Wayts

Willard H. Wayts

WILLARD HUDSON WAYTS: Seaman First Class, U.S. Navy. He was born February 6, 1910, in Upshur County. He was inducted February 18, 1944, and was honorably discharged November 24, 1945. He served USNTS, Great Lakes, Illinois, Const. Batt's. USNCTC, Wim, Virginia, APA Receiving Station, Receiving Barracks, Seattle, Washington, NAS, Astoria, Oregon, and USS *Sanborn* (APA-193). He was awarded the American Theater Ribbon, Asiatic-Pacific Theater Ribbon with two Service Stars, and World War II Victory Medal.

WINTEN L. WAYTS: Private, U.S. Army. Honorable Service in the Armed Forces of the United States of America. "This is to certify that Private Winten L. Wayts died while in the Service of our Country as a member of the Army of the United States on the 22nd day of August 1951. This certificate is awarded as a testimonial of Honest and Faithful Service." He was a brakeman on a train that was carrying troops and supplies to the front lines in Korea.

Winten L. Wayts

DORN EVERTT WESTFALL: Sergeant, U.S. Army. He was born April 24, 1946, at Queens. He was honorably discharged

August 14, 1974. He was awarded the following: National Defense Service Medal, Vietnam Service Medal with two Bronze Service Stars, Republic of Vietnam Campaign Medal, Bronze Star Medal with V Device, Purple Heart Army Commendation Medal, Air Medal, Good Conduct Medal, Combat Infantryman Badge Sharpshooter (Rifle), and 2nd Class Gunner (M-60 MG).

Virgil D. Westfall

VIRGIL DANIEL WESTFALL: Motor Machinist's Mate Second Class, U.S. Navy. He joined the service July 27, 1942, and was honorably discharged November 26, 1945. He served NTS NORVA, 26 NCB, 36 NCB. He received the Good Conduct Medal and World War II Victory Medal. He was discharged from Bainbridge Naval Station, Maryland. He died January 14, 1970, at Perry Point Hospital, Maryland. He is buried in the Heavner Cemetery in Buckhannon.

Robert E. Whitmoyer

ROBERT E. WHITMOYER: Private First Class, 2514th Service Command Unit, U.S. Army. He was born August 22, 1923, in Lebanon, Pennsylvania. He entered active service February 10, 1943, and was honorably discharged on March 13, 1946. While serving he received the following: Good Conduct Medal, American Theater Ribbon, and World War II Victory Ribbon.

JACKIE RAY WILFONG: E-4, U.S. Army. He was born September 9, 1939, in Ten Mile, West Virginia. He joined the service on August 14, 1963, and was discharged on August 13, 1965.

Gene H. Wilson

GENE H. WILSON: Private First Class, U.S. Marine Corps, Marine Detachment, USN Disciplinary Barracks, Naval Station. He was born September 19, 1920, at Rock Cave. He enlisted March 14, 1944, and was honorably discharged December 21, 1945. He served in the Asiatic-Pacific Area from August 4, 1944, to April 29, 1945. He was wounded on Iwo Jima, Volcano Islands on March 11, 1945. He participated in action against the enemy at Iwo Jima, Volcano Island from February 19, 1945, to March 11, 1945. He was awarded the following: U.S. Marine Corps Honorable Discharge Button, Honorable Service Lapel Button, Purple Heart Medal, and Bronze Star Medal.

RONALD GENE WILSON: First Lieutenant, U.S. Army. He was born December 18, 1940, in Buckhannon. He entered the service on June 23, 1964 and was honorably discharged on June 22, 1966. While serving he received a Letter of Appreciation and the National Defense Service Medal.

Ronald G. Wilson

DAVID WILT: Sergeant, U.S. Army. He entered the service in 1969. He served with U.S. Army Vietnam Dog Training Detachment, 101st Airborne Division, 545th Special Weapons Company and one Armored Division. He received the National Defense Service Medal, Good Conduct Medal (Third Award), Army Commendation Medal, Vietnam Service Medal, and Vietnam Campaign Medal with three Stars.

David Wilt

ERWIN EDWARD WINES: Sergeant, U.S. Army, Company B, Fourth Engineering Battalion (C). He was born February 25, 1933, in Syracuse, New York. He entered the service on February 12, 1968. While serving he was awarded the following: Good Conduct Medal with Fifth Award, Vietnam Service Medal with six Bronze Service Stars, Purple Heart, Bronze Star Medal with V Device, Army Commendation Medal with one Oak Leaf Cluster, Meritorious Unit Citation and two Overseas Bars.

Charles E. Wood

CHARLES E. WOOD: Private First Class, U.S. Army. He was born February 9, 1922, in Century, West Virginia. He was inducted on March 8, 1943, and was discharged on December 17, 1945. He served in Rhineland and Central Europe. While serving he received the Good Conduct Medal, World War II Victory Ribbon, the American Theater and the European-African-Middle Eastern Ribbon.

ALLEN RICHARD WRIGHT: Corporal, U.S. Marine Corps. He was born February 3, 1919, at Alton. He enlisted on September 27, 1943, and was honorably discharged on May 17, 1946. He served in the Pacific Area from September 19, 1944, to May 6, 1946. He participated in action against the enemy at Iwo Jima, Volcano Islands from February 19, 1945, to March 16, 1945, and in the occupation of Japan from September 22, 1945, to April 18, 1946. He was awarded the Good Conduct Medal.

BOBBIE WORTH ZIRKLE: E-2, U.S. Marine Corps. He was born March 17, 1947, in Buckhannon. He entered the service December 26, 1967, and was retired by reason of physical disability. While serving he received the National Defense Service Medal, Vietnam Service Medal with one Star, Vietnam Campaign Medal with device, and Purple Heart.

Bobbie W. Zirkle

ISHMAEL W. ZIRKLE: Private, U.S. Army, Company A, Eighty-sixth Chemical Mortar Battalion. He was born December 28, 1917, at Beans Mill. He was inducted April 22, 1941, and honorably discharged September 29, 1945. He served in Central Europe. He was awarded the following: European-African-Middle Eastern Theater Ribbon with one Bronze Star, Asiatic-Pacific Theater Ribbon, American Defense Service Medal, one Service Stripe and four Overseas Bars.

Ishmael W. Zirkle

Japan Surrender Ends World War II

Surrender of Japan on stern terms laid down by the victorious United Nations has brought to an end the most horrible and most costly war in the history of the world. Japan goes down in utter defeat as did Germany, Italy and other Axis Powers which once conspired to rule the world.

Toyko first informed the Allies she was ready to surrender, but she insisted that in the offer, the Emperor be allowed to keep all of his royal powers and rights.

Washington replied for the Big Four and said they were willing to accept a surrender of Japan under the terms of the Potsdam Declaration, but the Emperor must take his orders from the Allied Supreme Commander in Japan. Hours passed before Tokyo radio announced the Allied terms had been accepted.

Emperor Hirohito made a public announcement to the Japanese people that Japan, the nation which once could boast that it had never lost a war, had surrendered to escape "obliteration." The Atomic Bomb, he said, was the final instrument of Japan's defeat.

This was the most costly conflict in lives and monies of all times. World War II involved all nations on the globe except Spain, Sweden, Portugal, Switzerland and a small place known as Eire (Ireland).

The United States totals were 251,424 dead and 44,960 missing. Germany estimated 3,600,000 dead, Russia 5,300,000 dead, Great Britain 5,320,000 dead and 560,000 missing, China 1,500,000 dead and 100,000 missing, Japan at least 2,000,000 dead, besides the dead there were around 6,000,000 permanently crippled.

A break-down in expenditures of Allied Nations: Russia spent $170,000,000,000, Great Britain $64,200,000,000, France spent $13,000,000,000, South American countries $10,000,000,000, Germany $258,900,000,000, Italy $94,000,000,000 and Japan spent $44,000,000,000. No historians were able to obtain figures as to the amount China spent in this war as of 1946. The United States had spent $280,000,000,000.

The total cost of this war was over a trillion dollars and 30,000,000 lives lost.

All of the above figures were based from 1934 to the surrender of Japan in August of 1945.

This information was submitted by Charles S. Waugaman, quartermaster of Post 3663, Buckhannon, West Virginia.

Sergeant Edmondson Phillips Tells of Seventh U.S. Cavalry's Last Stand

Veteran of Five Wars Served for 34 Years in Regular Army.

Fighting Indians in the West was all in a day's work for Sergeant Edmondson Phillips, 89, of Alton, who served in the Regular Army of the United States for 34 years, seeing service in the Civil War, Indian campaigns, Spanish-American War, Boxer Rebellion and Philippine Insurrection. Sgt. Phillips began his military activities March 3, 1864, when he enlisted in the Union Army at the Courthouse at the age of 17 years. He was assigned to Co. M of the 3rd West Virginia Cavalry. Although the war was near its end, Sgt. Phillips saw much service in the Valley of Virginia during Hunter's Raid. At Lynchburg, VA, the 3rd Cavalry engaged in its first major conflict. At Moorefield, Sgt. Phillips and several of his men narrowly escaped capture, by the Confederates and were forced to hide for an entire day while a large force of the Southern army passed through the town. When peace was established after the surrender of Lee at Appomattox, Sgt. Phillips and his men were mustered out of the service June 2, 1865, at Wheeling.

Edmondson Phillips

Re-enlisted in Infantry

Seven years later he re-enlisted in the infantry on March 18, 1872, and was sent to the West where he became involved in one of the most famous episodes of American History. The American Government was experiencing great difficulty with the Indians at that time and sent a small army to subdue the savages. The force was placed under the command of General George Armstrong Custer, and Sgt. Phillips was one of the soldiers under the famous officer. Fortunately for Sgt. Phillips, Custer divided his force into four separate groups and set out in search of tribesmen. Sgt. Phillips was a member of the force under the command of a Col. Gibbons. Some days after the division of the army, rumors were rampant concerning the activities of the Indians and other divisions of the army. One night word arrived at the camp of Col. Gibbons that the 7th Cavalry under General Custer had met disaster. Sgt. Phillips stated that little was thought of the matter, but the three regiments under Gibbons were ordered to fall in and they set out in search of the cavalry regiment.

Discover Bodies

They marched for several hours and from time to time heard the call of bugles. Feeling that something was amiss, the regiments continued their march and as the morning sun appeared over the plains, they found the missing 7th Cavalry. "There was a heavy fog that morning," said Sgt. Phillips. "As it began to rise, the first thing I saw was a bright red object. I investigated and found that it was the skull of a soldier who has been scalped. The blood on his head made it glisten like a red mirror in the early morning sunlight. As the mists cleared we saw the bodies of men lying about. Some of them were warm, others had tiny sparks of life left in their bodies. In one spot we counted 37 soldiers. They lay in perfect formation, just as they had fallen in battle. Each man was in his proper place. A short distance away we found the remainder of the command. They were lying on top of a small hill." It was here that Custer had made his last stand. He was surrounded by the bodies of his men.

All Scalped

"Every soldier we saw had been scalped and mutilated in some manner with the single exception of the Commanding Officer, General Custer. The only mark on his body was a small hole in the back of his head where either a rifle ball or pistol ball had penetrated. Close by was the body of Tom Custer, brother of the general. The Indians had not only scalped him, but had cut his heart from his body and tramped it in the earth." We at once set out in search of the Indians who were still close by. The regiments were deployed as skirmishers and we advanced over the plains in a mile-long line, making an imposing array as our rifle barrels and bayonets glistened in the sun. "Our advance took us through an Indian village, the largest I had ever seen. In the distance we could see Indians riding to the call of bugles. They marched out and counter-marched in cavalry formations exactly as regular troops in celebration of their victory. They fell back as we advanced, however, and did not attempt to fight. In a short time we came to another hill and there was another part of the army surrounded. The Indians left as they saw our approach, and the besieged soldiers ran down the hill to greet us. They had been standing off their foes for three days without food or water. Many of them were so overjoyed they wept. We had little food with us, but divided what we had with the rescued troops."

Is Wounded

The remainder of the Indian Campaigns were uneventful, but in 1898 the United States declared war on Spain and Sgt. Phillips was sent to Cuba. From there he went to China where the Boxers, a patriotic Chinese organization, were conducting a campaign of extermination against all foreigners. He was a member of the force which rescued the besieged nationals in the Legation at Peiping. When the Philippine insurrection broke out, Sgt. Phillips was sent to the Philippine Islands and fought against the famous Aguinaldo. It was during this campaign that Sgt. Phillips received his first wound, an injury to his hand,

and the mark can still be seen. The Philippine Insurrection wrote finis to the long years of military service for Sgt. Phillips. He had passed the age limit, and when the World War began was too old to again don his uniform for active service.

Upshur County Veterans Entering Service During World War II Period

Three hundred eighty-eight Veterans entered during this period: Lee Browning Coleman, Charles Edward Coleman, David D. Casto, Jr., Herbert Clark, Neal F. McKisic, Garth Ben McKisic, Clarence Robert Gregory, Gaynor Woodrow Bean, Paul Clark Bean, John Nolan Hall, John Jonas Elbon, James Robert Nesbitt, Charles William Roberts, Jack S. Roberts, James R. Kelley, Henry M. Curry, Olin Gerald Malcomb, Franklin Noel Malcolm, Ernest Simons, John J. Kriner, Ralph P. Reppert, James E. Reppert, William Rinard Talbott, Hugh Thomas, John Edwin Burr, Cornelius C. Albaugh, Jr., Denzil Clayton Baxa, Gilbert Lervy Baxa, Carl F. Aylestock, James Edwin Aylestock, Woodford Samuel Aylestock, Russell Warren Aylestock, Charles Robert Hawkins, Ira Franklin Hartman, John Ramus Holtz, Morgan Ancel Patterson, Wilson Chester Harper, Willis Gerald Phillips, Orval S. Payne, Claude Clark Ours, Eugene Tenney, Phay Edward Tenney, Richard Lee Ours, Louis Everett Alderson, Paul Poundstone, Jr., Marple C. Hornbeck, Dan R. Hornbeck, Charles Hornbeck, Ira Jewell Beeson, Vern Earl Osburn, Carl Junior Beeson, Eugene Carter Davis, Robert Grant Strader, Elbert Clinton Powers, John Carl Waugh, Henry Otis Talbott, Davis McCoy, George R. McCartney, William A. Miller, Karl Harrison Trippett, Douglas C. Talbott, Lowell Lee Queen, Edgar Kenneth Prine, Arthur Reese Loudin, Jonathan Arden Crites, Gail J. Phillips, Herbert William Pugh, Errice Nazelrod, Jr., Dayne Edward Jack, G. O. Quertinmont, Mason E. Darnall, Charles Hulbert Grove, Harold D. Potter, Arthur Howard Hiner, Lester Harding Simons, Robert Oden Kittle, Howard James Knabenshue, Oscar Frank Anderegg, Charles Ishmael Moss, Ward D. Eakin, Roy T. Reeder, Charles Kincaid,

Joseph Ercel Kincaid, William G. Echess, Rue Shreve, Marvin Camden Zickefoose, Vendell Creed Tenney, Ulysses Grant Young, Llewellyn Boyd Allender, Carey Warren Allender, Allen Allman Allender, William Henry Underwood, Henry Leonard Tenney, Clarence Arthur Rice, Don Oscar Thomas, Othar Rowan, Herbert Rowan, Gerald Rowan, James Herbert Smith, John Porter Trembly, George Albert Smith, Annie M. Smith, Yvonne Rohrbough Miller, Sexton Linger, Rex V. Naylor, Charles William Smith, Ural Blaine Kellison, Rex Lambert, T. A. Berry, E. M. "Kuffy" Karrickhoff, Virgil Daniel Westfall, Robert Madison Westfall, Basel Carpenter, Gilbert Clyde Warner, Henry Hartzel Warner, Earl Williams, Odgen Warner, Harley C. Smith, William Howard Smith, Jess William Hinkle, Carrol Lee Smarr, Donald E. Reed, French A. See, Thomas L. Stockert, Jr., Conrad Maxwell St. Clair, Phillip Reese, Richard Lynn Byrne, Walter Cogar, Robert Burns Bailey, Hunter Audra Long, Robert Ray Long, Joseph W. Jeffcott, Ralph "Dutch" Travis, Garland Bruce Tomblyn, Zeward Copeland, Oliver Copelan, Roy M. Click, John Paul Linger, Reuben Ovid Linger, Edward Stephen Linger, Darius Wayne Crites, Mark Coyner, Jr., Leo Wilt, Kidd Lockard, Doris Franklin Craven, Paul Hardling Bailey, Jansen D. Wereley, Donald Edsel Cutright, Bernard Earl Werner, Robert Arnold, Marvin F. Linger, Albert Leroy Abel, Jesse B. Crislip, Deward Andrew Harman, Carl Talbott, Ben Hull, Archie Glass, Edward Huffman, R. H. Slaughter, Paul William Armstrong, Robert Junior Anderegg, David Marple Cartwright, Doyle Richard Carpenter, George Elliot Curry, Ray Junior Crites, Kermit Barrickman, Clifford Westfall, Paul Westfall, Herbert Newton Westfall, Myron Derwood Westfall, Brunson Williams, James Oren Smith, Boyd Brent Smith, Troy O'Brien Ware, John Hamilton Waugh, Clyde I. Waugh, Charles J. Poundstone, Ralph T. Spicer, Oren Earl Lane, Herman Denver Lane, Virgil Lee Lane, John D. Samples, Richard S. Smallridge, Hayes B. Smallridge, Morris Odbert Gillispie, Cleophas C. VanGilder, William Dayton Westfall, Noel Wilson Casto, Mason S. Hicks, William Bane Hicks, Jr., Hugh Edward Woodford, William Waggy, Jr., William Burk Douglas, Clatis Austin

Dean, Wilmer Dean, John Davis Cain, Charles F. Bennett, Jack Leon Davis, Brooks Davidson, Doyle Dean, Hubert Clinton Ensor, Harley F. House, Arthur Ford Kidd, Robert Lee Bloom, Jay A. Samples, John W. Long, Lyle Hoylman, Forrest Stump, Harry H. Hinkle, James E. Heavner, Richard Lynn Byrne, Oliver Fiery Harne, Russell Randolph, Bland Raikes, Marshall J. Reger, Carl Aylestock, Dewey Hoover, Charles Wilson Harman, Randolph A. Lane, Robert Burton Lee, Rex B. Reed, Kenneth K. Stanley, Richard Slaughter, William Harold Slaughter, Wilbur Earl Grose, Jimmy Brown, Woodford Post, Charles Henry Powers, Delbert Clinton Powers, Harrison W. Quick, William Roscoe Quick, Jerald E. Goodwin, Kenneth Orr Phillips, Forrest D. Queen, Bryan "Red" Moore, Raymond Hartman Samples, James E. Westfall, Kelsel Elwood Morgan, Charles Willard Reynolds, O. Beecher Phillips, Edgar Kenneth Prine, Edgar Quentin Miles, Howard Max Phillips, James K. McKisic, Donald J. McKisic, Sexton M. Linger, Lambert Harold Pumphrey, James Dolan Lewis, Sterlie William Light, Forrest Mayford Lake, Leonard Paul Ulderich, Kiser Tenney, Frank Earnest Hall, Reatice Loy Fultz, William E. DeTurk, Howard Winston Reppert, Leonard Brooks Reppert, Hoy Smith, Burl Smith, Ruel Gail Smith, Marble L. Zickefoose, James Riley McHenry, Oneal E. Riggleman, Edwin Gawthrop, Jr., Silas Earl Tenney, Roland Bonner, Forrest W. "Dick" Talbott, George Royden Vaught, James Marvin Beer, T. A. Berry, Cecil A. Thomas, Allen Young VanTromp, Tye V. Veith, Pearley Monroe Carpenter, Robert Lee Crites, Thurman L. Cochran, Jesse Lee Starkey, Marvin Jacob Crites, Ercel Ray Powers, Floyd E. Butcher, Richard Lee Butcher, Lynn E. Butcher, Carlos K. Butcher, W. Carl Naylor, C. Stanton Reed, Arthur Bunn Simmons, John T. Fitzwater, Charles "Bus" Fitzwater, Harold Starkey Pettit, Charles H. Osburn, Victor A. Osburn, Jack P. Lewis, Perry Carl Lewis, Glenn Ours, Parker Naugle Karickhoff, Theodore Norris Karickhoff, Wilbert Grim, Bacel E. Long, Ernest Keith Hosaflook, Glenn Richard Hosaflook, Kenneth Emory Moore, Edward P. Marteney, Howard F. Lance, Ben J. Strader, Forrest Roy Bean, Orval R. McCauley,

William Stewart McCauley, Orris Dayton McCauley, Donzel L. Hinzman, Rupert R. Strader, Fred Paul Strader, Denzil C. Hull, Richard Harper Brake, Edward P. Cutright, Frank Schroeder, Marshal Homer Trusler, Arthur Gordon Trusler, Kyle Elwood Miller, Nathaniel Jack, Marvin Lee Greene, Homer Shreve, Jr., Johnie Q. Leigh, Virgil F. Leigh, Lollive H. Leigh, Charles Jason Johnson, Meredith Edward Riggs, James K. "John" Myers, H. Hayden Morgan, Ross Lee Pringle, Earnest Earl Lantz, George H. Dixon, William A. Hallam, Claude Aldon Lewis, Ted Fowkes, John Randolph Clay Russell, Richard Keith Reeder, Robert Nick Ratcliff, Robert Wright Teter, Lorentz Ralph Bennett, Don Junior Casto, Carl Edward Casto, John Samuel Casto, Richard Brooke Neely, William Grant Brohard, Steward Tallman, Morris Virgil Tallman, Max Jackson Pifer, Gohen Arnold Pifer, Sherald Perry, John Paul Murray, Richard Patrick C. Murray, French Walton, Richard Charles Smallridge, Creed Grove Norman, Sewell Clair Phillips, Burl N. Shaw, Carl Royce Phipps, James Wade Phipps, Kenneth Steurer, Charles William Smith, Orlo Garland Smith, Clayce Keith Queen, O. B. Zirkle, Jr., Sidney Wade Gillispie, H. J. Lloyd, Jr., Fred W. Lloyd, Glenn Bond, Hunter Audra Long, Robert Ray Long, Russell Guy Andrick, Joseph Andrick, Floyd Allman Brinkley, Donald Dean Steele, Frank Bailey, John D. McCue, William D. Foster, Vernon French Friend, Charles Earl Reger, Jr., Bernard Harding Chidester, Ingram Junior Smith, Geraid Lock Smith, Kenneth Sands Stewart, Archie G. Teets and Cecil Alkire.

Honor Roll—Veterans of Foreign Wars—Post 3663

Spanish American War

Spalding Winchester.

World War I

Arden A. Andrews, Frank B. Bartlett, Bryon L. Bennett, Arthur D. Brady, Oaky L. Bragg, Andrew Buchanan, Lloyd W. Carpenter, Amon Cutright, William F. Dean, Newton Dumire, Lidle C. Facemire, Paul Fidler, Forman H. Goodwin, Loy J. Halterman, Joseph H. Hornbeck, Hugh House, Pearley B. Howes, Cecil C. Hyre, James F. Loudin, Charles M. Perry, Frank A. Reger, Lawson D. Regester, Howard Rowan, Clifford K. Stockert, William P. Smith, Austin S. Taylor, Marcellus C. Tenney, Benjamin D. Wagner, Joseph Wagner and Hobart C. Wilfong.

World War II

Cecil Minter Alkire, Llewellyn Boyd Allender, William Anglin, Ward Bailey, Roy Lovon Ball, Maxell R. Barnett, Daris Paul Bean, Dorfie Wm. Black, Jennings Black, Sherald Perry Brady, Charles R. Brown, Jack Burner, James Burner, Richard L. Byrne, Paul Carpenter, Robert E. Claypole, McKenzie Craig, Doris F. Craven, Bernard M. Criss, Charles Crites, Darius Wayne Crites, Jonathan Arden Crites, Robert Crites, James C. Curkendall, French DeBarr, Odell S. Davidson, Hartzel Dean, Henry Edgell, French Eskew, Wm. D. Findley, Richard B. Fowkes, Wm. H. Halterman, Roy E. Hawkins, George F. Hoover, Sherley M. Hornbeck, Lewis Eugene Johnston, Joe Ercel Kincaid, Margel Landis, Marple Landis, Goff Leroy Lanham, Wallace Owen Leigh, Wm. Kyle Liston, Archie E. McGray, J. R. McDermott, Glenvil Roy McDonald, Charles

Thomas McKisic, Albert E. Miles, Ova Ralph Miller, Ralph Nesbitt, Victor Osburn, Herman Kenneth Phillips, Wm. Wirt Phillips, Wilmer G. Poling, Roscoe Prince, Lowell Lee Queen, Donald Reed, Richard K. Reeder, Denzil Roby, Chalmer Harding Rohr, Sammy Tenney Rowan, Charles B. Shreve, Denver Shreve, Donald Paul Simmons, Paul Russell Smith, Walter W. Smith, Edward Tenney, Vet Eugene Tenney, Herbert Thomas, Goff Jr. Tomey, Ralph E. Travis, Robert Waggy, Carl J. Wagoner, Hayward Lee Wagoner, Alvin F. Walton, Oran Odel Walton, William Warner, Woodrow Warner, James Norton Waugh, Verl Zickefoose Williams, Nelson M. Wilson, Freddie Whiters and Arnold G. Zickefoose.

March, 1942—Registrants Get Calls to Report for Examinations

Largest Group of Draftees Will go to Clarksburg For Final Army Physicals During Next Week.

A. H. Lawson, clerk of the local draft board, today issued a tentative list of Upshur County registrants to be examined by the Army Examining Board at Clarksburg next week. The list follows: Glenn Gates Hartman, William Henry Underwood, George Edward Fagons, Gilbert Leroy Baxa, Burlen Chesley Zickefoose, James Andrews Dean, Allen Young VanTromp, Ernest Scott Andrews, Oscar Dean, Charles Ivy Wise, Glenn Willard Miller, Ophie Linger, Abram Lawson Gaston, Garlton Gay Adams, Enos Dean, James Robert McDermott, Theadore Hite Fowkes, James Richard Kelley and George Robert Kent, all of Buckhannon. Edward Ansel Green, John Randolph Clay Russell, Charles Earl Reger, Jr., Wilbur Roy Booth, Fred Coy Ware, Grover Creed Norman and Junior Zickefoose, all of Adrian. John Dayton Samples, Clovis Charles Brake and Kemp Crawford Brake, all of Rock Cave. Virgil Daniel Westfall, Alston Gordon Jackson, Thomas Payne Hawkins, Seigal Clark Rollins, French Herbert Miller, Claude C. Rollins, Ray William Reed and Glenn Junior Linger, all of Route 4, Buckhannon. Oval McKisic and Harry Hartsel Walton, both of Kanawha Head. Duran Paul Gifford and Darius Deering Moreland, both of RFD, Buckhannon. Jefferson Davis Ashcraft, Thompson Javis Brooks, Russell Wilson Smith, Forman Ralph Howes, Oral Loyd Lower, Howard Jonathan Dowell, Jessee Bee Crislip, and Oscar Frank Anderegg, all of Route 3, Buckhannon. Donovan Marshall Wingrove of Hemlock, James Arthur Cooper of Ingo, Sherley Clofa Koon, Harold Ward Bailey and Arlton Glendale Adams, all of Tallmansville. Richard Charles Smallridge and Charles Willard Zickefoose, both of Alton. John Harley Miller, Steward Tallman

Arthur French Miller, Ova Ralph Miller, Dellot Earl Hornbeck and Charles Lewis Hornbeck, all of Route 2, Buckhannon. Alexander King Loudin of Route 1, Buckhannon. Lowell Carl Phillips, Reatice Loy Fultz, Patrick Henry Reeder, Sewell C. Phillips and Denver Charley Brady, all of Route 1, French Creek. Floy Gap Shipman, Leonard Willis Herron and James Oren Smith, all of Queens. Major Lee Hinkle and William Paul Ward, all of Route 2, Hall. Blaine Browning, Delbert Glenn Jack, Boyd Odell Booth, Harry Vincton Crawford and Arthur Lee Harris, all of Route 1, Hall. Russell Tolliver and Guy Darl Combs, both of Frenchton. Argel Denzil Neely and John Francis Shoulders, both of French Creek. Edgar Glenn Helms, Daris Paul Bean, Robert Lyle Rice, Elmer Denzil Gregory and Fred Paul Strader, all of Canaan. Dane Ervin DeBarr of Ten Mile. Robert Lee Reeder and William Everett Newcome, both of Imperial. Bland Raikes, Denzil Arty Liston and Delbert Glen Sanders, all of Arlington. Henry Martin Curry and Claude Hayes Winemiller, both of Alexander, Paul Lee Reger and Kermit Olen Hosaflook of Route 1, Alexander, Curgie Charles Davidson of Gaines, Oskar Williams of Abbott and Joe Van Hamner of Sago.

Upshur Countians Entering Service 1942-43

This is a list of some of Our Upshur County Boys that went into the Service in 1942 and 1943: Four brothers were serving at the same time. They were the sons of Mr. and Mrs. P. S. Aylestock. The oldest was Pfc. Carl F. Aylestock. He was stationed with Co. D, 115 Infantry, 29th Div. in England. He was inducted in May of 1941. Pfc. James Edwin Aylestock was stationed at Fort Sam Houston, TX with the H. Q. Co., 1st Bn., 9th Infantry. He was inducted June 30, 1941. Sgt. Woodford Samuel Aylestock was in Co. E, 6th Q. M. Training at Camp Lee, VA. He was inducted in October 1941. The youngest enlisted in July of 1942. He is Russell Warren Aylestock. He took training at a government radio school in Washington, D.C. Wilson Rinard Talbott, aviation metalsmith, 2nd Class. He is the son of Mr. and Mrs. W. G. Talbott of W. Main St., Buckhannon. He enlisted on Feb. 25 and was stationed at Norfolk, VA. Pvt. Everett Hugh Thomas, son of Mr. and Mrs. Hugh Thomas of French Creek, WV was in the Repair Squadron of the Army Air Forces in England. He enlisted on October 25, 1941. Cpl. John Edwin Burr, son of Mr. and Mrs. Floyd Burr of Adrian was inducted on Feb. 17, 1942, in the Army. He served in Battery C, 306c. A. B. B. B., 188th and Doty Ave., Hawthorne, CA. Cpl. Frank Joseph Feola, outstanding basketball player at B-U High School and Wesleyan College, entered the service on May 13, 1942. He is the son of Mr. and Mrs. Sam Feola. He was a physical education instructor with the Army Air Forces at Sioux Falls, SD. Cpl. Oscar Lloyd Friend, son of Mr. and Mrs. L. T. Friend of Canaan, WV was stationed at Camp Rucker, AL with a tank unit. Sgt. J. Paul Carpenter was a parachute instructor at New River, NC with the U.S. Marines. He is the son of Mr. and Mrs. J. W. Carpenter of Buckhannon, WV. He enlisted

July 2, 1936. William Page Ball, Machinist Mate, 2nd Class, U.S. Navy, was a survivor of U.S.S. *Wasp* aircraft carrier, that was torpedoed and sunk on Sept. 15, 1942. He enlisted July 7, 1940. He is the son of Mrs. Dove Ball, Buckhannon, WV. Cpl. Mason E. Darnall, son of Mr. and Mrs. T. A. "Eck" Darnall of Buckhannon was stationed at Camp Polk, La. He enlisted Feb. 3, 1942. Pvt. Jansen D. Wereley was stationed in Northern Ireland with the U.S. Army. He is the son of Mr. and Mrs. Edward C. Wereley, Buckhannon. Donald Edsel Cutright was with a Radio School, IMIOW-15, U.S. Navy A.S. (SS) at Jacksonville, FL. He enlisted July 9, 1942. He is the son of Mrs. Ida M. Cutright of Buckhannon. Pvt. James K. "John" Myers, U.S. Marine Corps. He is the son of Mr. and Mrs. Wade Myers of Buckhannon. Mayor of Buckhannon before entering the service, Sgt. Thomas L. Stockert, Jr., is stationed with the 5th Service Command at Ft. Hayes, Columbus, OH. His wife Joyce S. Stockert resides in Buckhannon, WV. Cadet Marvin Lee Greene enlisted in the Army Air Forces on May 6 and was furloughed until Oct. 21, when he was sent to Nashville, TN. He is the son of Mr. and Mrs. Guy W. Greene of Buckhannon. Edwin Gawthrop, Jr. was a junior instructor in the U.S. Army at Biloxi, MI. He formerly taught general science at B-U High School. He enlisted on Sept. 7, 1942. He is the son of Mrs. Mamie Gawthrop of Buckhannon. 2nd Class Petty Officer George Royden Vaught was stationed with the 20th U.S. Naval Const. Bn. in Camp Rousseau, Hueneme, CA. He enlisted in the U.S. Navy on June 1. Trusler Brothers, Pvt. Marshal Homer and Pvt. Arthur Gordon. They were inducted on Sept. 10 and May 13 respectively. The boys nearest relative is their grandfather, Marshall Bennett of Buckhannon. Pvt. Marshal Trusler was at Camp Lee, VA and Pvt. Arthur Trusler was at the Station Hospital, Camp Barkeley, TX. This is the way it was reported in the Buckhannon newspaper in 1942 and 1943.

Deceased World War I Upshur County Veterans

Newton Anderson, Thurman Andrew, Simon Ashcraft, Carl C. Bailey, O. L. Barrackman, Cecil Brown, John W. Brady, Frank B. Bartlett, Earl C. Congleton, Armour Cookman, J. Park Caynor, Taylor Cowger, James W. Cockerill, John Cockerill, Rev. Wilson Crites, Charles W. Courtney, W. C. Douglas, Dana Dean, Clifford Francis, William Earl Fultz, Quick Fumerola, T. C. Fisher, Francis Fitzgerald, H. C. "Tuck" Farnsworth, Hilbert Ford, Henry A. Fidler, Goff W. Ervin, Sam Feola, Sr., Eddie Fretwell, Sr., Fred Foster, Victor F. Brady, Ralph S. Brady, Orville A. DeBarr, Emanuel H. Crites, Charles Gibson, Frank W. Gould, E. J. Gaunt, Sisco Griffith, Marvin Green, C. H. Grove, Ben L. Hull, E. Page Harris, Irl M. Humphrey, Jas. L. Harvey, John Ruskin Hall, Duffy Hornbeck, Sr., Ezro Halstead, Glenn F. Ireland, Cecil E. Johnson, E. J. Jorishie, Wm. G. Kiddy, Alpha E. Koon, Frank M. Kellar, Bernie Kincaid, O. L. Kesling, Darius Lewis, Hugh W. Linger, I. Ray Light, John W. Lesure, Earl Loudin, Simon R. Layfield, Paul B. Lewis, Voris S. Mearns, A. Dodd Morgan, Leslie R. Miles, O. G. McCue, George McArthur, O. W. Morris, Charles Morris, O. B. Phillips, S. O. Phillips, P. Clifford Post, Columbus I. Post, John Post, Jesse Pifer, B. M. O'Donnell, Clete Queen, Clifford S. Reeder, Dr. J. A. Rusmisell, Sr., Guy Ross, Kelcel Ross, Willie Russell, Clifford Royer, V. C. Ruhlow, Homer P. Rohr, Roff Rundio, Lawrence See, Herbert P. Stalnaker, Charles F. Short, Augustus M. Sexton, F. Guy Strader, G. W. Steerman, W. T. Stockert, Freeman D. Simmons, Raymond Scott, Clifford Stockert, Monzel Shipman, John B. Scott, Leslie R. Simons, Wm. H. Snodgrass, Columbus Teets, Bert. T. Tenney, Leslie Vangilder, Charles D. Ward, Samuel R. Warner, Edward C. Wereley, Charles J. White, Fred Wilfong, David S. Young,

James A. Zickefoose, Wm. H. Zickefoose, Wm. Zoeffel, Selby Waugh, Walter Wilde, Troy O. Ware, E. L. Williams, J. A. Ware, Rev. M. A. Workman.

Upshur County World War I Veterans Still Living

William Andrew, Harold T. Bailey, George H. Dixon, Myron B. Hymes, Sr., Doy Jack, Victor Earl Mick, Richard Phillips, Stanley Kellison.

Cemeteries
Deceased Upshur County Veterans

Mt. Nebo Cemetery

Lionel Armstrong, Dorsey Bloom, Jacob Campbell, Londa Campbell, Albert Halterman, Jacob Carl Lesure, John Lesure, Chester William Linger, Joseph McDermott, Jesse Musgrave, Abram Rucker, Edward Shaffer, Francis Shamburg, Denver Shreve, Sylvester Shreve, Robert Sipe, Lyda Suder and Dan Williams.

Heaston Ridge Cemetery

Dwight Allman, Albert Alkire, Arden Andrew, Ray Andrew, Troy Andrew, Dorfie Black, William Boggs, Otis Casto, William Claypool, Everett "Bud" Currence, Howard Currence, Cecil Houghton, Elias Houghton, Joe Houghton, Willard "Jack" Houghton, Abner Hunt, Alva O. Hunt, Isaac Hunt, John Hunt, Henry Jeffries, Reuben Jeffries, Clarence Loudin, J. D. Loudin, John Loudin, Willard Loudin, Eugene Mick, Charlie McKisic, Everett Perrine, Lon Perrine, Lester Pritt, Roy Reynolds, Amos Samples, Bryan Samples, John Peter Salamon, Clarence Sampson, Robert Ware and William West.

Union Cemetery

Jacob D. Henderson, Benjamin Hornbeck, John Kittle, Smith Kittle, Jas. P. K. Koon, Samuel A. Lane, James E. Montgomery, Jed Nay, Aquilla Osburn and William Ray.

Sand Run Baptist Cemetery

Randolph S. Anglin, James M. Black, Rufus Blake, Gay Booth, Gilbert C. Booth, Lee Booth, Sterling W. Campbell, A.

F. Carr, Harley Caynor, Alonzo Cutright, Clark Cutright, Lorenzo H. Cutright, Reuben Crites, Dewey Dawson, William Douglas, William Fallen, Foreman Goodwin, Blanda L. Hallar, Raymond Harris, George W. Hess, Blondie Hollen, Fay E. Hollen, Paul Hollen, Raymond R. Hollen, Victor P. Hollen, Bayard Jack, Charles B. Jack, John W. Jack, Delbert Glen Jack, Harry D. Keller, George Kelly, John Kelly, Lonnie Ralph Lace, Lonnie Lowe, Percy Merret, Bennie Noe, Ray E. Norvell, Charles I. Ocheltree, Franklin Ocheltree, George Ocheltree, Ralph Lewis Osburn, Jesse Pifer, Elmer A. Poling, Robert L. Riffle, Ralph Edward Roth, Charles See, Monzel Shipman, William O. Waugaman, Charles S. Whitacre, Junior B. Woodson and Eugene N. Whystell.

Alton Cemetery

George Detamore, Abraham Hosaflook, Henry Miller, Richard Hillery Walker Pringle, Daniel Wilfong and Minter J. Zickefoose.

Heavner Cemetery

Oscar C. Layman, Donald A. Farnsworth, Archie F. Howard, Clifford A. Wagner, Donal W. Woodell, James Martin Manley, Stanley Davis, Charles B. Layman, Sherman E. Lambert, Morris S. Newlon, Franklin F. Morris, Charles C. Halterman, Clarence E. Watson, Larry Lee Morris, Dwaine E. Hornbeck, Hughey C. Westfall, Hilbert Ford, Darrell Martin Wilfong, Charles W. Courtney, Howard D. Furr, R. Lynn Dawson, Richard B. Walton, Arnell D. Riggleman, Edward L. Gould, Wilbur D. Harris, Nathan J. Rexroad, William Franklin West, Thomas Eugene Miller, Charles J. Poundstone, James Adams Russmisell, James A. Russmisell, Jay McKinley Tenney, Granville R. Yokum, Austin Creed Laymond, Minter E. Dennison, Casby L. Smith, Robert H. Smith, Wilbur G. Miller, Edward C. Wereley, Bettie Simpar Byers, Phay Edward Tenney, Eugene Tenney, Edward J. Gawthrop, John M. Slaughter, William H. Halterman, James J. Halterman, Robert Lee Clark, Raymond C. Post, Arkie Basil Bowyer, Cecil B. Ross, Homer Phillip Rohr,

Charles H. Hinzman, Robert H. Woodford, Marvin E. Lantz, Arbro F. Huffman, George L. McAuthur, Charles H. Bodkins, Ray Darford Clark, Sewell Clare Phillips, Forest Beer, James Lyndon Beer, James Henry Alfred, William E. Phillips, Kyle Wm. Gimmel, George Bland Edmiston, Clarence E. Westfall, William B. Mallonee, William Roy Mallonee, Hess Skidmore, John S. Steele, Camden W. Holden, George R. Heavner, William J. McKinister, Willie J. Phillips, Ernest Cutright, Sisco U. Griffith, Charles Sheets, Homer Lee Mercer, Sylvester E. Waugh, James B. Tenney, Sterling G. Lantham, Harold W. Pickens, Russell H. Fox, Paul E. Crumrine, Jr., Freeman Strader, Hubert Clinton Ensor, William R. Bunner, Gorden D. Furr, Orvalle E. Jeffries, Hugh Wallace Simons, Burl N. Shaw, David Frank Scott, John Bogue Scott, Odgen Warner, Quick Fumerola, Daniel Gorden Simmons, Garner W. Groves, Guy C. Combs, William H. Barlow, Woodrow W. Corder, Robert C. Combs, Jack Robert Hyre, Ralph S. Chandler, George Osten Bailey, Jr., Roy C. Cunningham, Charles B. Bailey, Guy Joseph Douglass, John E. Knabenshue, John William Long, Fred Harold Hollen, C. Woodford Marsh, Stanly E. Butcher, William Oscar Windom, Bert F. Windom, Daryl Windom, Paul Edison Thomas, Henry Allen Fidler, Archie Baxter Bennett, Hartzel Huff Johns, Mearl Ours, Loman Wesley Paugh, John Russell Powell, John N. Powell, Moody B. Tonkin, John F. Phillips, Jr., Doy S. Ratliff, Harrison L. McCoy, Aaron Minter Duncan, L. G. Demastes, Otto J. Simmons, Lavere D. Ritter, Richard F. Talbott, Hugh W. Linger, Henry A. Taylor, Russell Lyle Neely, Gilbert Henry Booth, Maxell E. Zickefoose, French C. Kepner, Arthur H. Smith, Oscar Guy McCue, Willie Ours, Leo Frank Hyre, Paul James Carpenter, William C. Calling, A. Lincoln Ashworth, Lawrence C. Henry, Cecil Phillips, William B. Hicks, Jr., Cecil Goff Brown, Richard Lynn Byrne, Augustus Macavoy Sexton, D. Pitt O'Brien, Creel S. Cornwell, Sr., Oliver C. Mitchell, John M. Slaughter, Edwin J. Gawthrop, Robert H. Smith, James Alfred Meadows, Robert N. Ratcliff, Ishmael G. Cutright, Jr., Ronald L. Fenstermacher, William D. Keller, Bennie J. Hibbs, William Hamilton, John Clifford Royer, Kenneth H.

Waugh, Randall L. Post, Rex. B. Reed, Homer Dean, Troy O'Brien Ware, Okey William Morris, Ray Lynn Arbogast, Aubrey T. Warner, George W. Short, James Russell King, Mason P. Cutright, Clemens K. Steurer, Harry J. Moore, John Joseph Chipps, Taylor T. Cowgar, John S. McMurdo, Ronald L. Kesling, Torlock Rasmussen, Edward James Mackey, Paul G. McKissic, Harold Denver Slaughter, Russell Pritt, Floid E. Travis, Ralph E. Travis, George Albert Smith, F. Haymond Rollins, William C. Phillips, James Henry Alfred, James Lindon Beer, Joseph P. Hall, Robert Addison Layfield, Stillman Orr Phillips, Richard Lee Young, Marley C. Tenney, Richard C. Hope, Donald R. Stalnaker, John Grill, Jr., Israel Ray Light, James Lake Ellis, Jr., John M. Cockerill, Earnie Lee Hopkins, Mildred Kathleen Eckess, William G. Eckess, James H. Kerans, Randy Layne Long, Clarence F. Hiner, Clark M. Whiting, Herbert P. Stalnaker, Odbert W. Williams, Doyle W. Williams, Doyle F. McCord, Verlin O. Marple, Asa Thomas Waugh, Adam Harold Martin, E. Page Harris, Edward B. Spicer, Wilmer Dean, Everett R. Simons, Hartzel Henry Asper, Frank Bailey, Audra F. Cottrill, Jake Ferguson, John A. Stockert, Daniel N. Cutright, Woodford Post, French W. Dean, Kyle E. Miller, Mark Coyner, Jr., Earl S. Moore, James D. Hinkle, Jr., Hartzel E. Dean, Manuel Leffler, William W. Wagner, Yale M. Canfield, Richard R. Cross, Jr., Duren Burl Harman, Willie D. Woofter, Thelma M. Moore, Opha Liman Kesling, Charles G. Zickefoose, Paul Henry Kesling, Russell C. Pritt, Floid E. Travis, Ralph E. Travis, George Albert Smith, S. F. Haymond Rollins, Donald A. Farnsworth, Clifford A. Wagner, Donal W. Woodell, Sherman E. Lambert, Charles B. Layman, James R. Farnsworth, Stanly Davis, Roy Junior Slaughter, James Martin Manley, Morris S. Newlon, Franklin F. Morris, Charles C. Halterman and Wilbor G. Miller.

First place—Mountain State Forest Festival, 1957.

Honoring our dead at Post 3663, Buckhannon. *Left to right:* Morris Ringer, Joey Slaughter, William A. Lewis, and Sewell Phillips.

VFW Post 3663, Buckhannon. *Left to right:* Junior Mackey, Joey Slaughter, Stanley Grose, James Gladwell, Richard Young, Cap Harvey, William Jack, Gordon Chapman, Charles N. Taylor, Warren Simmons, Edward Mackey, Russell Neeley, John Phillips, Erlo Peterson, Morris Newlon, and Charles Shaffer. *Standing on monument:* Don Junior Casto, Sewell Phillips, and Dillon Swick.

Upshur County draft to Camp Lee, Virginia, September 3, 1918.

Installation of officers—Ladies Auxiliary VFW Post 3663, Buckhannon. *Front row, left to right:* Mona Mackey, Eulah Snyder, June Godwin (Elkins), and Ruby Cox. *Second row:* Grace Swick, Janet Carpenter, Helen Ringer, Wanda Lamb, and Virginia Smith. *Third row:* Frances Carter, Icie Smallridge, Sandy Armentrout, and Phyllis Ours.

Ladies Auxiliary, Buckhannon Post 3663. *Left to right:* Ruth Casto, Nellie Guth, Geneva Dowell, and Minnie Fawcett from Grafton. *Second row:* Grace Swick, Francine Quertinmont, Rita Lewis, and Marie Sharpolisky. *Third row:* Betty Cox, Vera Kelley, and Ava Kittle.

Voice of Democracy. *Left to right:* Mary Alice Thurman (teacher), Sarah Jane Heater, Max Guth, Gordon Chapman, and Frank Feola.

VFW Post 3663, Buckhannon. *First row, left to right:* Charles Posey, Richard Ours, Blaine Godwin, and Charles Waugaman. *Second row:* Retice Hinkle, Gerald Phillips, Evert Smith, Clifford Loudin, Morris Ringer, Neff Casto, and Winfred C. ("Bud") Alkire.

VFW Post 3663. *First row:* Ivan Hodges, Evert Smith, Retice Hinkle, and Paul Ellison. *Second row:* Denver Caynor, Max Guth, Noel Casto, and Richard Young. *Third row:* Morris Ringer and Clifford Loudin.

VFW Post 3663, Buckhannon. *First row:* Edward Shaffer, Gerald Phillips, Clyde J. Dalton, and Eugene Walker. *Second row:* Junior Mackey, Frankie Casto, Dick Young, Charles N. Taylor, and Edward Mackey. *Third row:* Russell Neeley, Charles Shaffer, William R. Jack, and Herbert H. Price.

VFW Post 3663, Buckhannon. *First row, left to right:* Frankie Casto, Clyde J. Dalton, Edward Mackey, Gerald Phillips, and Richard Young. *Second row:* John Phillips, Junior Mackey, Eugene Walker, Charles Taylor, Aubrey Heflin, (Dept. Q.M.). *Third row:* Charles Shaffer, William Jack, Morris Ringer, and Russell Neeley.

Arthur Simmons, *left;* Nathaniel Jack, *right.*

VFW Post 3663, Buckhannon. *First row, left to right:* Gordon Chapman, Michael Sharpolisky, and Herbert, Jack. *Second row:* John Slaughter, Richard Cooper, Clifford Loudin, Retice Hinkle, Max Guth, Junior Mackey, Morris Ringer, and Edward Mackey.

Some of the boys at Post 3663 relaxing and having a good time. *Front row, left to right:* Richard Young, Yale Canfield, John Phillips, Russell Neeley, Earl Martin (playing piano), Charley Shaffer, and Gaylord Armstrong. *Back row:* Gerald Phillips, Morris Ringer, Clyde J. Dalton, Edward Mackey, and Forrest Stump.

VFW Post 3663, Buckhannon. *Seated, left to right:* Mason Darnall, Michael Sharpolisky, and Max Guth. *First row:* John Slaughter, Junior Mackey, Morris Ringer, James Faucett (Past State Commander), Retice Hinkle, Richard Heatherly, and Gerald Phillips. *Second row:* Clifford Loudin, Gordon Chapman, Neff Casto, and William R. Jack.

VFW Post 3663, Buckhannon. Edward Wereley, *left;* Frank Bailey, *right.*

VFW Post 3663, Buckhannon. *Seated, left to right:* Forrest McAtee, Retice Hinkle, and Richard Heatherly. *First row:* Frankie Casto, Junior Mackey, Russell Neeley, and Richard Cooper. *Second row:* William R. Jack, Paul Westfall, Clifford Loudin, and Edward Shaffer.

VFW Post 3663, Buckhannon. *Seated, left to right:* Richard Cooper, Herbert Jack, Gordon Chapman, and Michael Sharpolisky. *First row:* Edward Mackey, Morris Ringer, John Slaughter, and Retice Hinkle. *Second row:* Junior Mackey, Clifford Loudin, and Max Guth.

Monument in front of Upshur County courthouse.

Trophy display case in meeting room at VFW home. Awards to VFW from community group who VFW has sponsored and helped.

VFW—viewed from exterior on Kanawha Street.

Life members for permanent charter. *Front row, left to right:* Burton Morland, Joe Wilt, Charley Posey, Junior Rollins, Sewell Phillips. *Back row, left to right:* ?, Morris Ringer, Gordon Chapman, Woody Marsh, Don Casto.

Original Firing Squad, VFW, 1947. *Left to right, first row:* Bud Lewis, Hayse Baughman, Harry Hinkle, Sherd Tenney, Bus Simmons. *Second row:* Junior Mackey, Earl Hawkins, Jim Kittle, Carius Campbell.

Left to right, first row: Hubert Jack, Richard Heatherly, George Groves, Clifford Loudin. *Second row:* ?, Retice Hinkle, Richard Cooper, Gerald Phillips, Richard Young. *Third row:* Max Guth, Morris Ringer, Mason Darnall.

Dave Casto band in 1949. Members shown are: Dave Casto, trumpet; Bob Gainor, saxophone; Don Adams, trombone; Buck Shahan, guitar; Andy Clark, drums; and Jack Fields, piano.

Disabled American Veterans, Pringle Tree Chapter No. 5 officers. *Left to right, seated*: Senior Vice-Commander Ernie Towell, Commander Billy Joe Mackey. *Standing*: Chaplain Nathaniel Jack, Adjutant and Treasurer Warren Hosaflook, Second Junior Vice-Commander Virgil Anderson.

Mountain State Forest Festival in 1963. *Left to right*: Junior Mackey, Bill Levere, Charles Taylor, and Jim Kittle.

Addendum

YALE M. CANFIELD: Tech. 4, U.S. Army. He was born May 30, 1911, at Frenchton. He entered active service on February 17, 1944, and was honorably discharged on October 25, 1945. He served in Rhineland and Central Europe. While serving he received the Purple Heart Medal with Oak Leaf Cluster, Good Conduct Medal, Croix DeGuerre with Palm, Distinguished Unit Badge, and European-African-Middle Eastern Service Ribbon.

Yale M. Canfield

Frank J. Feola

FRANK J. FEOLA: Staff Sergeant, 3704th Army Air Forces Base Unit. He was born Oct. 18, 1919, in Pickens. He was inducted on May 13, 1942, and was honorably discharged on December 11, 1945. While serving he received the American Theater Ribbon, Victory and Good Conduct Medals.

DAYNE EDWARD JACK: Son of George W. and Cathrine Jack, was born on August 17, 1916. He was inducted in January 1942. He served twenty-seven years in Seoul, Korea. Retired to USAR Control Group USAAC, St. Louis, Missouri. While serving he received the Armed Forces Expeditionary Medal, Good Conduct Medal (sixth award), National Defense Service Medal with one Oak Leaf Cluster, Vietnam Service Medal, and Vietnam Campaign Medal with Device 60.

Homer H. Martin

HOMER H. MARTIN: Son of Mr. and Mrs. C. J. Martin of French Creek. He served in the U.S. Navy from July 7, 1942, to November 13, 1945; Boot Camp, Norfolk, Virginia; Aviation Machinist Mate School, Jacksonville, Florida; Scouting Squadron 69, Pearl Harbor, Hawaii; Engine Overhaul, Kaneohe-Oahu, Hawaii; C.A.S.U. 32, Santa Rosa, California; Aviation Carburetor School, Chicago, Illinois. He was in the Clarksburg Fire Department for 21 years. He worked for the U.S. Postal Service in Springfield, Virginia, for 19 years. His present address is 9907 Loudoun Ave, Manassas, Virginia 22110. He married June Tenney of Hesper, West Virginia; they have three children and three grandchildren.

GAIL PHILLIPS: Son of Mr. and Mrs. Loyd Phillips of French Creek, was wounded in action in New Guinea on July 3, 1943. The War Department reported his condition as favorable. He was able to write to his parents on July 18 to tell them he was getting along all right. Private Phillips was inducted into the service August 14, 1942, and has been overseas since October 1943. Before his induction he was employed by the Diamond Alkali Company at Painesville, Ohio. He had a brother in the service, Sgt. Willis G. Phillips, who was located in Normandy.

WILLIS G. PHILLIPS: Sergeant, Co. B, 270th Engineering Battalion, U.S. Army. He was inducted on May 13, 1943, and honorably discharged on October 21, 1945. He served in Normandy, Northern France, Ardennes, Rhineland, and Central Europe. While serving he received the Good conduct Medal and European-African-Middle Eastern Service Ribbon. He was born July 11, 1909, in French Creek.

Willis G. Phillips

Arnel L. Pomp

ARNEL L. POMP: He was born in Adrian, Upshur County. He was inducted March 8, 1943, in Clarksburg. He served eight months and three days before being honorably discharged from the Pasadena Area Station Hospital in Pasadena, California, on November 20, 1943.

RUSSELL SMITH: U.S. Army. He was inducted on March 28, 1942. While serving he was in Australia Brisbane, New Guinea, Admiralty-s, Leyte, Luzon, Philippine Islands, Manila, Honshu Island, Japan, Yokohma, Tokya, and Meijei Shrine Park, Tokyo, Japan. He was discharged November 3, 1945.

BERT SPENCER STEWART: Corporal, regular army. He was born November 17, 1932, in Buckhannon. He entered the service on July 7, 1950, and was honorably discharged on July 6, 1953. While serving he received the Korean Service Medal with three Bronze Service Stars, United Nations Service Medal, and Distinguished Service Unit Citation.

LLOYD C. STEWART: Private, 803 Pio. Infantry 4 B & S Dt. He enlisted on August 4, 1918. He served in Meuse-Argonne. While serving he received Medals, Badges, Decorations, Citations, and the Victory Medal. He was honorably discharged on July 24, 1919.

LLOYD C. STEWART, JR.: Private First Class, 3999th Quartermaster Truck Company, U.S. Army. He was born January 7, 1926, in Buckhannon. He entered active service on February 15, 1944. He was honorably discharged on April 21, 1946. While serving he received the Asiatic-Pacific Theater Ribbon, Good conduct Medal, Meritorious Unit Award, and the Victory Medal World War II.

Arthur G. Trusler

ARTHUR G. TRUSLER: U.S. Army, Staff Sergeant, 900th Base Depot Company, Transportation Corps. While serving he received the Asiatic-Pacific Campaign Medal and Ribbon, American Campaign Medal & Ribbon, Good Conduct Medal, Philippian Liberation Ribbon with one Bronze Star, and World War II Victory Medal and Ribbon. He was honorably discharged on January 16, 1946.